MW00626048

TALES OF A

MADMAN

Chris, "Back Enjoy my to the Future" take on advertising in the digital world.

Archie

Cover Design by Randy Titchenal
www.behance.net/randletitc8c79

Interior Layout by Yolanda Ciolli

ISBN 978–1–942168–94–2 Hardback
ISBN 978–1–942168–95–9 Paperback
ISBN 978–1–942168–95–9 eBook

Library of Congress Control Number: 2019905658

Published by
Compass Flower Press
Columbia, Missouri
www.CompassFlowerPress.com

TALES OF A

MADMAN

Advertising Secrets for Success in the Digital World

Archie J. Thornton

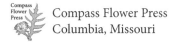
Compass Flower Press
Columbia, Missouri

For Gail, my wife of nearly three decades, for her enduring love and support of my journey through the advertising and technology industries.

Dedication

To my business associates, friends, and mentors who helped guide my career and helped me learn valuable advertising lessons:

Alex Hern, **Bill** Phillips, **Bob** Bernstein, **Charlie** Reeb, **Dick** Parker, **Frank** Haas, **Gary** Kelly, **Graham** Phillips, **Jerry** McGee, **Joel** Raphaelson, **John** Blaney, **Ken** Roman, **Martin** Sorrell, **McAvoy** Layne, **Paul** Peterson, **Phil** Kinnicutt, **Ray** Williams, **Roger** Morey, **Ross** Jasper;
and *the late* ***Bill*** *Calhoun,* ***Bob*** *Haldeman,* ***Bobbye*** *Hughes,* ***Chuck*** *Pebbler,* ***David*** *"D.O." Ogilvy,* ***Jack*** *Roberts,* ***John*** *"Jock" Elliott,* ***John*** *"McDee" McDermott,* ***Tom*** *Kemp, and* ***Whitey*** *"M.O." Lee.*

Contents

Preface

What do you get when you cross *David Ogilvy on Advertising* (1985) and *Forrest Gump*? You get TALES OF A MADMAN: deep insights about how advertising works and intriguing scenarios with just about every advertising and brand great you've ever heard of. The author is savvy, scrappy Archie Thornton, an advertising executive and entrepreneur who has a lot of opinions about how to handle the challenges of the transformation of advertising in the digital world. These opinions are supported by real world successes. If you have a creative student in your advertising class, are training young recruits in an ad agency, or wonder how to enhance your career in advertising as it exists today, this is the book for you. Thornton's career is textbook on how serendipity can be turned into marketing success. *Enjoy.*

—Esther Thorson
College of Communication Arts and Sciences
Associate Dean for Graduate Studies
Michigan State University
Fellow of the American Academy of Advertising

Introduction

The Fourth Industrial Revolution

"This is not about entertainment or just playing video games. This is a different way of interacting with the world, a new generation of computers."

—Thomas Tull
Founder of Legendary Entertainment
Forbes Magazine

I believe augmented and virtual reality technology will usher in the Fourth Industrial Revolution. Both will fundamentally alter the way that we live, work, and interact with each other. It will replace many of the technology tools that we employ today. AR and VR will revolutionize media distribution.

This seismic event will be characterized by a fusion of technologies that will blur the lines between the physical, digital, and biological spheres.

Goldman Sachs, in a recent industry report, predicted the market for AR and VR hardware sales will outpace the sales for televisions in annual revenue by 2025, generating over $110 billion in annual sales.

Unfortunately, the term VR has become a generic term for many different technologies and capabilities. To grasp the potential for developments in this immersive world, you must understand the different technologies that make up this broad category.

- **Virtual reality** is just one component within the category. In its most basic form, it replaces the real world with a computer generated, three dimensional image or simulated environment and allows the users to interact with it.
- **Augmented reality** is a separate technology that allows you to superimpose a computer generated image on a user's direct or live view (in real time) of the real world, creating an enhanced, composite world.
- **360–degree viewpoint** technology produces a spherical photograph or video that surrounds the viewer in every direction. It can include either recordings or live video streaming. It only immerses the viewer in the environment and does not allow for interaction.

According to Kevin Kelly, in his book *The Inevitable,* interaction and presence are propelling the VR industry:

"Presence is what sells VR. All the historical trends in cinema technology bend toward increased realism, starting from sound, to color, to 3–D, to faster, smoother frame rates. Those trends are now being accelerated within VR. Week by week, the resolution increases, the frame rate jumps, the contrast deepens, the color space widens, and the high–fidelity sound sharpens, all of it improving faster than it does on big screens."

Most of us in the advertising, entertainment, or gaming industries have likely tested the immersive, virtual reality experience through headsets introduced by Facebook (Oculus), Google Glasses, HTC (Vive), Samsung, or Sony.

If you have played Pokémon, you have experienced augmented reality in its most basic form. But, the real game changing technology is being pioneered by companies like Magic Leap. Magic Leap's immersive experience is currently delivered through a tethered, head mounted display. Eventually, the final product will fit in a pair of glasses.

This development could usher in a new computing dimension and create the next generation interface, or a kind of contextual computer. This new device could project an image directly onto your retina through a revolutionary optics system built into semi-transparent glass. This technology will replicate the way we normally view our world.

This system will also constantly gather data by scanning the room for obstacles, tracking hand and eye movement, and listen for voices. In the industry, we call this process SLAM, or Simultaneous Localization and Mapping.

Disruptive technology will impact every business that relies on screens and computers. According to David M. Ewalt in *Forbes* magazine:

> *"It could kill the $120 billion market for flat-panel displays and shake the $1 trillion global consumer-electronics business to its core."*

The technological impact on advertising will cause many to rethink the traditional ways we approach creating and delivering our content and message.

Ewalt predicts, *"...you can throw out your PC, your laptop and your mobile phone, because the computing power you need will be in your glasses, and they can make a display appear anywhere, at any size you like."*

Ewalt cites everyday examples relating to the future of reality. For example, one future change could be having the directions to your next meeting appear in yellow lines on the road ahead of you or being able to transport a new couch right into your living room and view it from every angle under every lighting condition *before you buy*.

Even those of us that are not mechanically inclined will be able to repair our automobiles or appliances, utilizing an interactive program with alerts to notify when we are doing something incorrect.

Heather Bellini, the respected Goldman Sachs Analyst for Media, Technology and Telecommunications industries, has called augmented and virtual reality, "...the next generation computing platform."

Bellini is describing a disruptive technology. Technology that doesn't only do new things, but rather, will change the way that we do everything. For example, the smartphone has been one of the most disruptive technologies. Ten years ago, most people didn't even own one; now it is something that is integral to your daily life.

According to Bellini, both AR and VR are paving the way for another device where the controls are largely driven by head and hand movements.

Certainly, there will be other disruptive technologies besides the transformational and immersive advances that will directly impact how advertising messages are created and delivered.

Artificial intelligence (AI) will be able to aggregate and analyze your personal information to the point where advertisers will be able to deliver commercials that predict your individual desires before you can imagine them.

In–home digital assistants will have the ability to systematically customize information you request and then direct you towards products that advertisers have paid it to promote.

This sophisticated type of *digital spying* and use of big data will control what consumers see and hear. Advertisers will be able to gain access to these targeted prospects.

All the advertising secrets I will introduce in this book will become relevant as we try to harness the potential of this new virtual media as it permeates our real, everyday world.

Chapter One

Simple Secrets for Success

"In the coming two decades, the challenge and opportunity is to harness filtering technologies to create higher quality of attention at scale."

—Kevin Kelly
The Inevitable

I retired from Ogilvy & Mather at forty-seven years of age. David Ogilvy was the same age when he founded the agency.

For the last two decades, I have been actively immersed in the evolving role technology is playing in everyone's lives and how advertising helped fuel that growth.

I have been a marketing advisor to venture capital firms. I have managed successful and unsuccessful startups. And for the last five years, I have been active as an individual investor and board member in several ventures.

Such efforts have created my personal net worth which grants me the freedom and opportunity to continue to seek out new prospects and provide advice and counsel to new ventures and growth–oriented companies.

This net worth is certainly nowhere near the headline grabbing wealth of entrepreneurs such as Mark Zuckerberg of Facebook, Larry Page of Alphabet (Google), or Elon Musk of Tesla, but I consider it a princely sum.

While most personal wealth has been generated from my work and investments in technology, success has been built on a solid foundation of advertising principles I grew to embrace during my decades in the agency business.

> The only real change is the nature of the media in which the message is delivered.

How these Secrets Apply in the Digital World

What I have learned during this adventure is that the basic principles of advertising David Ogilvy preached during his tenure at Ogilvy & Mather still apply. The only real change is the nature of the media in which the message is delivered.

Experience is a Good Teacher

Rather than boring you with my detailed perspective on these principles, I am going to take you on a tour of my nearly three decades in and around the world of advertising. On this tour, I am going to chronicle some of the major episodes of my career and how real–world experiences helped me learn valuable lessons.

Alongside my story, I will outline for you why I believe these principles still apply today and how these simple lessons can help you succeed and profit in today's digital world.

Chapter Two

How Advertising Changed My Life

"Don't tell my mother that I work in Advertising, she thinks that I play piano in a whorehouse."

—John "Jock" Elliott
Chairman, Ogilvy & Mather International
Senior Account Management Program, 1982

I was going to be a pilot. It was always a given. I grew up in Kansas City, north of the Missouri River. Many of my friends' fathers and neighbors were pilots for Trans World Airways.

The TWA headquarters was located in Kansas City. As a young boy, the prospect of working just a couple weeks a month and playing golf the balance of the time was appealing.

On my sixteenth birthday, my dad agreed to pay for my flight training.

When I enrolled at the University of Missouri, I knew I was only there to punch my ticket and obtain the college degree needed to be a pilot. My primary focus centered around my role as social chairman of my fraternity and working part time at Woody's, the local traditional men's clothing store. I started working in menswear retail in high school. I found it a rewarding challenge to help customers improve their wardrobes, while also improving the looks of my commission checks.

It was the late sixties and the war in Vietnam was heating up. Student deferments from the draft were disappearing. To avoid the inevitable, I applied to the Advanced ROTC program the Air Force was offering for potential pilots. I could already fly, so passing the flight aptitude tests weren't a challenge.

> I was going to be a pilot. ...When I enrolled at the University of Missouri, I knew I was only there to punch my ticket and obtain the college degree needed...

The program demands were manageable. After acceptance into the Advanced ROTC program, applicants had to attend a six week basic training course between their sophomore and junior years at university. Besides the basic military indoctrination, the course included an introduction to fixed wing flight school, jet orientation, small arms instruction and survival training.

During the course year, the only requirement was to attend a one hour class each week that focused on refining presentation or briefing skills. All-in-all, it was an ideal solution for my situation and future. I was out of the draft and upon graduation I would be commissioned and assigned to jet training called the Year of 53 Weeks.

Career Plans Grounded

Plans were moving along smoothly until I shattered my wrist falling out of my window in a bone–headed fraternity–house incident. I was granted a military deferment and promptly given an honorable discharge from the Air Force. My well–planned career in aviation was grounded.

Good Advice, Great Luck

Until then, I hadn't been faced with declaring a major. I decided to seek the counsel of an advisor. After a brief conversation, the advisor reviewed my transcript, which was nothing to write home about. She noticed I seemed to perform better in courses more focused on written work.

Her next suggestion surprised me. She pointed out the University had the only School of Journalism in the country and its reputation for turning out graduates with real world experience was exceptional. Upon her recommendation, I applied and was later accepted.

The first semester at the journalism school consisted of an introduction to the general principles of journalism and acquiring the basic skills of the profession such as reporting, editing, and photo journalism. After that semester, you were required to declare your sequence of study. The major options included a focus on advertising, broadcast, or newspaper course study. I chose advertising. I really don't know why. Perhaps, because I thought that the job Darin had in the television sitcom, *Bewitched*, looked interesting.

Real World Training and Experience

To my surprise, I loved the curriculum and the hands-on approach of the program. That included turning out graduates with experience in advertising sales for the local community newspaper, the Missourian, and the local NBC affiliate, KOMU, writing copy for the ads that were sold, and developing and designing the newspaper or magazine layouts. Before I knew it, I had graduated with a Bachelor of Journalism degree.

I hadn't thought much beyond my college education. During my final semester, I interviewed with several companies who visited campus. I was most interested in the New York based, J. Walter Thompson account management training program. JWT is now a wholly owned subsidiary of the advertising and public relations giant, WPP, who also owns Ogilvy & Mather.

> . . . working for an advertising agency is like completing an MBA in entrepreneurship.

My father, who was a manager at the Kansas City operation of Owens Corning Fiberglass, had wrangled me an interview with both the marketing and public relations departments of the company in Toledo, Ohio. While I didn't know it at the time, the advertising agency for Owens Corning was Ogilvy & Mather, which had created the famous "Pink Panther" advertising campaign for their building insulation products.

No Rush to Succeed

Since I wasn't being pressured by any military commitment, I wasn't ready to jump into a long time career commitment either. My father couldn't understand my lack of motivation. He had grown up during the depression and survived World War II as a tail gunner on a B–17. He thought a college education was a privilege and a fast track to a rewarding career. I seemed like a coddled baby–boomer who had graduated with a prestigious degree during the Woodstock era.

After many heated debates, I was able to convince my dad I needed a vacation after my four years of study to figure out what I wanted to do with my life. He agreed to underwrite a holiday trip to Hawaii with a classmate of mine named Charlie Reeb. The only condition was when I ran out of money, I was to telephone him collect and he would send me a one–way ticket to Toledo.

My Takeaway

On the surface, the lesson here appears to be *it's better to be lucky than smart.*

But, after over three decades in and around the advertising business, I have come to believe working for an advertising agency is like completing an MBA in entrepreneurship.

Advertising is one of the few businesses where new recruits are regularly exposed to a multitude of different products and services, unique and varied target audiences, and any number of specialized distribution channels and issues.

If you can take advantage of rare opportunities to spend quality time with clients, delve into the unique aspects of their business models, and understand this potential for your own personal growth, you can open your horizons to new paths for career satisfaction and success.

The Quadrangle at Mizzou

My Flight Squadron at Maxwell AFB

Chapter Three

Aloha to Advertising

"Your role is to sell, don't let anything distract you from the sole purpose of advertising."

—David Ogilvy

Since we knew little about the Islands of Hawaii, Charlie and I decided to book travel to the Island of Kauai. Our decision was based partly on the fact that Elvis Presley had filmed a movie there and Charlie had a friend he had served with as a Marine in Vietnam.

His friend, McAvoy Layne, had a job as a D.J. at the only radio station on the Island. His wife managed a small condominium complex in a vacation rental pool. Happy to see an old friend, they put us up in an unoccupied condo in exchange for help around the property.

Our planned few week adventure stretched into a couple of months. We both fell in love with the tropical lifestyle and collectively vowed to never leave. Unfortunately, we had run out of money.

Leap Before Looking

It was decision time. I had to find a job or call my father. Unless cutting sugarcane appealed to us, Kauai had limited job opportunities. All appealing options were in the big city of Honolulu, on the Island of Oahu.

Since Charlie's college career had been disrupted by Vietnam, I was the only one who had a marketable, college degree between us. We decided we would pool our remaining resources together, which consisted of a total of twenty–five dollars.

I would take the lion's share of our funds, fifteen dollars, and make my way to Honolulu. I used Charlie's military ID to book an inter–island flight on Aloha Airlines. It cost a total of seven dollars.

When I arrived in Honolulu, my strategy was to make my way to the newspaper offices and start my job search there. A four dollar taxi ride dropped me off outside of the Hawaii Newspaper Association offices. This left me with a grand total of four dollars in my wallet. Failure was not an option.

I entered through the impressive double doors of the art deco inspired building. What I didn't know was that this was the office of two competing daily newspapers. The Honolulu morning and evening newspapers had been granted unique permission to share a printing facility. Their independent editorial and sales staffs were both housed in this building in separate offices on the second floor.

Up the stairs to my right were the offices of the Honolulu Star–Bulletin, the evening newspaper. To my left, the offices of the morning paper, the Honolulu Advertiser. I decided to go to the right.

In 1969, there was a small-town feel in Honolulu. The business community was very friendly and accessible. I asked the receptionist if I could see the managing editor of the paper.

She simply said, "Let me see if he is available." When she put down the phone, she told me that he was on the telephone and that he could see me when he finished the call. She escorted me through the newsroom, which looked a lot like the newsroom for the *Missourian,* the university-staffed daily newspaper where I had studied. Rows of desks with reporters hunched over manual typewriters were seen along the way. In the background, there was the consistent hum of the teletype machines of the Associated Press and UPI. Around the perimeter of the room, there were glass offices for the various departmental editors. The office of the managing editor was at the far corner of the newsroom.

The receptionist offered me a seat right outside his office. From the bench, I could read a plaque on his desk. It read: A. A. 'Bud' Smyser. He was holding the phone to his ear with his shoulder while he typed away in a two-finger style, reminiscent of old film noir movies.

Here I was, sitting outside the office of the managing editor of a major Honolulu newspaper. I had no resume, no writing samples, and no plan.

Education Opens Doors

While he continued to talk and type, my eyes roamed to the wall behind him. It was filled with framed awards, pictures of famous people, and various commemorative plaques. Then, I noticed it. A 1969 Journalism Week Award for the Best Front-Page Layout from the University of Missouri.

When I was ushered in, I introduced myself and complimented him on the award. He volunteered that he had enjoyed the trip to Columbia and the Journalism Week events.

Here's where my years of experience selling shirts and ties kicked in. I told Mr. Smyser I had been on the Islands for an extended trip and had decided to make it my new home. I told him I appreciated him taking the time to see me and I thought he might have some suggestions regarding employment. He stated he was going to have an opening in their sports department in a couple of weeks. Since I didn't think my four dollar reserve fund would tide me over until then, I told him I was really anxious to get started earlier.

After pondering my reply for a few moments, Mr. Smyser picked up the phone. I could only hear his side of the conversation. When he hung up, he told me he had spoken to a woman named Bobbye Hughes. She had recently opened up a new public relations agency in town and she was looking for a junior writer.

The managing editor of a major metropolitan newspaper had just set me up for an interview with a new P.R. firm called Communications Pacific. (It would later be acquired by Hill & Knowlton and become part of WPP.)

Two days prior, I had been thinking about a job cutting sugar cane. Today, I was in the office of the state's largest ad agency.

Mr. Smyser told me Bobbye Hughes's offices were just down the street on Kapiolani Boulevard, in the PanAm Building. I thought the aviation connection was a good omen.

I walked out of the newspaper building and looked right. The PanAm Building loomed in the distance. I would need my four dollars to eat on, so I set out on foot for my meeting. The distance of the building was like a desert mirage that looked closer than reality.

Halfway to my destination, the tropical skies opened with a midday shower. I was soaked when I arrived at my meeting. After apologizing to the receptionist for my appearance, I sat down in the air conditioned office and tried to dry off.

Good Chemistry

Entering Bobbye Hughes's office, I was immediately charmed by her laid back style and Texas accent. Overlooking my damp and disheveled appearance she said, "In Hawaii, we consider it a sign of good luck when it rains on your event."

After the icebreaker, we talked about growing up on the mainland and how we had become captivated by the Islands and its people. She asked about my personal interests, sports loyalties, and of course, favorite authors.

Miss Hughes wanted to know about my time at Mizzou and the J–school curriculum. She asked how they specifically used practical and real life experience in their course study. She also asked about my favorite professors. Somehow, she came away impressed with my academic credentials and passion for the profession. She said I would be a good fit for her new firm. But, before she could offer me a job, she wanted me to meet her partner and major investor. I was enthusiastic.

She called and left a message at her partner's office, explaining who I was and asked if he could take the time to interview me. Fortunately, his office was just across the street.

I was running on empty from not eating and I still had the four dollars in my pocket, but I decided to forego any stop for food and head straight for the interview. The offices of Fawcett McDermott were on the fifteenth floor of the Ala Moana Building, the headquarters for the Dillingham Corporation, one of Hawaii's big five.

The receptionist was friendly and stated Miss Hughes left a message for John McDermott, who was out of the office, but expected back shortly.

While I waited in the lobby, I had a chance to learn some background information on Fawcett McDermott. The company was the largest advertising agency in Hawaii and represented some major clients, including: Sheraton Hotels in Hawaii, Aloha Airlines, British Overseas Airline Corporation (now British Airways), Amfac (another of the Hawaii big five), Honolulu Gas Co., and the Hawaii Visitors Bureau.

Two days prior, I had been thinking about a job cutting sugar cane. Today, I was in the office of the state's largest ad agency.

My first glimpse of John McDermott was more of a study in motion. He was a dapper gentleman with flowing white hair, combed back in an aristocratic style. He was carrying a large, black presentation portfolio (later referred to as a *pizza bag* by the industry). He swept through the lobby, grabbing a stack of messages from the receptionist's hand.

Timing is Everything

After a brief interval, he reappeared with yet another presentation bag and stated he would be back in an hour. He disappeared down the hall into an elevator.

Later, I saw him returning and I decided to go on the offensive. I jumped up when he entered the lobby and announced that Bobbye Hughes had asked me to meet with him.

Mr. McDermott stated he received Miss Hughes's message and motioned to follow him into his office. While I was still standing, he sat down on the edge of his desk and asked me to tell him a little about myself.

I told him I was a graduate of the University of Missouri's School of Journalism and that I was a writer.

Apparently relying on Miss Hughes's assessment of my capabilities, he explained he needed a copywriter immediately because his senior writer had just quit to race in the TransPac Yacht Race from Long Beach to Honolulu.

Immediately forgetting my opportunity with the P.R. firm, I volunteered for the copywriting position. He replied, "We'll see. I'll start you at $115 per week and review you each Friday." I asked if the review was to see if I deserved a raise. He said, "No. It's to see if you get to stay."

John McDermott called out to his assistant to have the creative director come to the office. When he appeared, McDermott said, "See if you can find this kid a desk and typewriter. Give him that Sheraton job. Let's see what he can do!"

Simple Solutions are Best

That afternoon, I worked on the project with another writer and art director. On the surface, it was a complicated task—promote the fact that all five major hotels on Waikiki Beach were Sheraton Hotels.

The solution was in the headline:

> *"This Year, Go to the Beach.*
> *Sheraton's Beach.*
> *Waikiki."*

The headline was approved. My first ad would appear in national magazines like *Time, Newsweek*, and regional magazines like *Sunset*. I thought, *Hey, this is easy.*

Back Down to Earth

My next writing assignment wasn't quite so heady. It was writing pithy copy for the cocktail napkins used in the Banyan Court of the Moana Hotel (famous as the location for radio broadcasts by Arthur Godfrey).

You might not have thought there was a lesson in this story that would apply in today's digital world. But, you would be wrong.

David Ogilvy, in both his in-house agency training videos and best selling books on advertising, would say if you wanted to become a good advertising copywriter, you needed to spend six months selling shirts at Macy's on Herald Square and 34th Street.

The simple principle was echoed in the Ogilvy & Mather agency slogan:

> *"We Sell…or Else!"*

The advertising business in its most simplistic terms is convincing someone to buy your client's product or service. In the prior situations, I was selling myself; my capabilities, training, and potential.

In an interview with Inc.com in August 2017, technology innovator and billionaire, Mark Cuban was asked what he would do if he lost his fortune. Cuban said, "I would get a job as a bartender at night and a sales job during the day. Could I become a multimillionaire again? I have no doubt."

> You might not have thought there was a lesson in this story that would apply in today's digital world. But, you would be wrong.

Success is based, in almost any field, on solid sales skills. Skills should teach persistence, self–discipline, the ability to negotiate, and how and when to close a sale. These refined talents will project a level of confidence that leads to success.

Whether you are creating an ad for Facebook, tweeting about a new product feature, or delivering an elevator pitch to a potential investor, you are selling. Your success depends on your salesmanship.

I was fortunate because of my interest in traditional menswear, I had experienced years of retail selling, both at Mister Guy and Woody's Men's Store.

Do whatever you can to improve and refine your selling skills because they can be one of the most important keys to success. For most people, selling doesn't come naturally. To refine your selling skills, I recommend engaging yourself in selling situations whenever and wherever you can. Practice your selling technique by pitching copy ideas or media strategies to your co–workers.

If you are tapped to pitch an advertising campaign or advertising execution to a client, practice your approach and delivery style in front of your account team, friends or family.

Ask for their criticisms and take their suggestions to heart. No successful attorney would go to trial without testing their prosecution or defense strategies, opening statements, and closing arguments before a mock jury.

Don't assume you can succeed by only knowing your materials and the strategies behind your recommendations. Your selling technique must be fine-tuned to project your sincerity and conviction behind your recommendations. It is paramount your presentation style communicates your confidence in your solution.

Without my six years of early retail sales training in menswear, I might have ended up flying back to Toledo.

Clockwise from top:
Hawaii Newspaper Association Building;
Adam "Bud" Symser, Managing Editor, *Honolulu Star Bulletin*;
Bobbye Hughes McDermott, Founder,
Communications Pacific Public Relations;
John McDermott, Fawcett McDermott Advertising

Chapter Four

Content is Still King

"You cannot bore people into buying your product!"

—David Ogilvy

I loved living and working in Hawaii. During my first year at Fawcett McDermott I had gained invaluable experience in advertising and an introduction to the business of travel and tourism. I also talked my college sweetheart into getting married and joining me in Honolulu.

I was concerned, however, that I would always be considered the new kid at the agency. I needed to see if I could compete on a larger stage. When my wife announced that she was pregnant with our first child, I decided it was time to take the leap. So, I quit my job and we headed to Los Angeles to test the waters.

Auditioning on the Big Stage

After landing in Los Angeles, the first order of the day was to pick up the new Volkswagen that I had purchased by phone from Honolulu. We were able to stay with a relative while we got our bearings.

That first afternoon, I cold–called three leading agencies. Over the next couple of days, I met with some legendary West Coast ad men. The first meeting was with Bill Calhoun, an executive vice president at Young & Rubicam. Calhoun, as he liked to be called, headed up the large Kaiser Aluminum and Gallo Wine accounts. He later retired to the Island of Kauai and we became lifelong friends.

The second meeting was with Bob Haldeman, president of the Los Angeles Office of J. Walter Thompson. Mr. Haldeman, who ran the presidential campaign to elect Richard M. Nixon, later became famous as White House Chief of Staff.

My final meeting was with Jack Roberts, co–founder of Carson–Roberts. They had risen to prominence as the agency for the Barbie Doll. Later in the decade, they would be sold to Ogilvy & Mather.

In a weird twist of fate, all three of these agencies would later be acquired by my future employer, London–based industry giant WPP.

The interviews went very well and my prospects looked promising. Both JWT and Y&R called me back for second interviews. Haldeman even suggested some ways to improve my portfolio.

Carson–Roberts wanted to know if I would be interested in switching over to become a producer. I was elated. My wife was not. She had decided she wanted to be near her mother in Kansas City, Missouri for the birth of our first child. Leaving the glitter of Hollywood behind, we hit the road.

Small Market, Big Opportunity

I arrived in Kansas City, Missouri with no real connections in the agency business and no job prospects. What I did have was a reasonably impressive portfolio (greatly improved by Haldeman's suggestions) along with a three-commercial television reel.

I stumbled upon a classified ad by a local ad agency looking for a copywriter/creative director.

> The agency president, Bob Bernstein, was a creative, new business machine, who had big plans for the future. … They would later serve as the sole agency for Walmart for over thirty years.

The agency was a relatively new, fifteen person firm named Bernstein-Rein. They were looking for their first copywriter. They had been relying on the account executives to write copy. The creative department consisted of two art directors and one broadcast producer.

The agency president, Bob Bernstein, was a creative, new business machine who had big plans for the future. While the agency had a typical, small agency foundation of retailers and car dealers, Mr. Bernstein had set their sights on larger, more sophisticated consumer product accounts.

And they were well on their way to achieving that goal. Their growing client list included Marion Laboratories' Gaviscon, Wright's Liquid Smoke, Borg-Warner products, KalKan Dog Food and the McDonald's Restaurants in Kansas City. They would later serve as the sole agency for Walmart for over thirty years.

It was an interesting change–of–pace and challenge since my total work experience to–date had centered on travel and tourism.

No Small Accounts, Just Big Opportunities

I had been at the agency for a little more than six months when we acquired the advertising account of a small regional apparel manufacturer located in Fort Scott, Kansas. It was called Key Work Clothes. While their product line focused primarily on work wear for the factory or farm, Key was expanding into the booming blue jean category.

Key Work Clothes did not have a budget for brand advertising. Their ad spending was tied to co–op advertising programs to support their retail customers in small rural markets.

Since there was no real glamour attached to the business, Key became a sort of orphan account. The company was owned by a tight–fisted, crotchety old curmudgeon. But, somehow, we got along.

After the owner had given me the tour of a couple of his factories, he asked me if I would mind giving a guest lecture at their local college. I suggested that once we had his new advertising materials produced, maybe I could present a case study to the students. He liked the idea.

Since the budget and markets were so small, we recommended Key allocate 100 percent of their co–op funding support to local radio. In those days, radio ads were lovingly referred to as "a dollar a holler" in small markets.

Key had never used broadcast media, so the management and sales force were excited at the prospect. We produced a series of sixty second radio commercials with twenty–second donuts (holes) inside for the retailer message or offer.

Right Message, Right Media

It was hard to find a truly unique selling proposition for the Key product line. I hung the creative concept onto the all-natural trend being advocated by the hippie and flower-power generation.

We used a folk rock singer accompanied by a single guitar. The message was equally simple:

> Key Work Clothes. Hard-working clothes made of rugged, easy-breathing cotton. Made in the Country… for Country Folks like You!

The retailers loved the branding jingle and the commercial moved goods off the shelf.

> Now, like then, the right content, tailored for a specific audience and media, is the correct formula for success. …But, it is important to not let big data and technology tracking capability dominate the creation of quality content.

And, that crotchety old curmudgeon sat in the audience when I presented the case study at his local college. He was so pleased that he even bought me lunch afterwards.

The entire advertising budget couldn't have been much more than $150,000—but the results were big.

About two months after the campaign for Key Work Clothes was launched, I received a phone call from the vice president of sales for the H.D. Lee Company, headquartered in Shawnee Mission, Kansas.

Their longtime advertising director was retiring and they were looking for a replacement more in touch with the baby-boomer generation. He said that they had heard my commercial and they thought that I might be that guy.

Why Content Still Matters

When tasked with the job of creating an advertising program for Key Work Clothes, I needed to craft a message consistent with my client's product offering and brand reputation that resonated with their retailers and rural customers.

Now, like then, the right content, tailored for a specific audience and media, is the correct formula for success. The success of digital media is also built on a solid foundation of quality content. Certainly, advancements in technology have made it easier for people to communicate, collaborate, and search for information particularly relevant to their needs.

But, it is important to not let big data and technology tracking capability dominate the creation of quality content. When it does, the resulting content or advertising message produced can represent a formulaic approach where the data dictates a template solution or approach.

We must remember, in its most simplistic form, advertising is just storytelling. To deliver desired results, the story must convey a message that inspires action on the part of the user and presents the brand, product, or service in a favorable and memorable way.

The ever-increasing number of digital distribution options available today have created an environment intent on limiting any story to its predetermined fifteen seconds of fame. But, the best and most successful people in this business are relentless in their efforts to craft memorable messages with a longer lifespan. The most successful brands don't become bored with the retelling of their underlying stories. Over time, these stories will evolve in creative ways and adapt to changing habits and lifestyles, but the underlying premise will remain consistent. David Ogilvy used to say, "It is important to remember that when the client is getting bored with the creative, it is just beginning to work."

Within this ever-expanding universe of media options, it is more difficult to grab the consumer's attention. As a result, many companies are employing a technique that blurs the line between advertising and content. It is called *native content*. The idea is to deliver your message in a style that does not look and feel like traditional advertising.

Right Message for the Media

However, the challenge for the advertiser is the need to deliver their story in this longer, native content style relative to the brand and the consumer, but in a form that is appropriate for the host media.

> David Ogilvy used to say, "It is important to remember that when the client is getting bored with the creative, it is just beginning to work."

With all of the real-time data available to advertisers today, it is important to make the decision as to whether to have their story be presented in either a responsive or adaptive style.

Timely Content

By *responsive*, I mean having the ability to quickly tailor the message to events or trends that may influence the purchasing decision of the consumer. For example, if you are a retailer and your trading area is experiencing an unusually wet spring season, you may want to promote the benefits of your stock of umbrellas or rain gear rather than swimwear for the upcoming summer season.

Appropriate Content

Adaptive is a more challenging approach for most advertisers because it requires them to tailor their content to the style, tone, and manner of the host media. Simply, it requires the advertisers to adapt their message to the media's audience in a context appropriately interesting to them. For example, if the social media site delivers entertainment news and celebrity gossip, the advertiser's message should replicate a similar style. If the host media is a business oriented site, the tone and manner of the message should be adapted to present the message in a more serious manner that reflects the mood and interests of its audience.

The guidelines are simple. Keep it short. Keep it pithy. And strive to engage jaded viewers.

Visual Impact

When creating a message for today's increasingly, visually oriented audiences, a static message alone won't deliver the desired impact. Look on such image–based, social media sites like Instagram, Pinterest, and YouTube to see what is trending viral.

The guidelines are simple. Keep it short. Keep it pithy. And strive to engage jaded viewers. Your goal should be to hit a cultural nerve that stimulates conversation, sharing, and viral growth. Remember, you can't bore your audience into buying your product or service.

In today's digital world, the *big idea* needs to be particularly relative to the events or trends that could impact the sales of the product or service. It needs to be appropriate for the media in which it is delivered. David Ogilvy always said:

> *"It takes a big idea to attract the attention of consumers and get them to buy your product. Unless your advertising contains a* big idea*, it will pass like a ship in the night."*

Advertising is not something that can be fixed with fancy production values or spending levels. The lesson learned has always been that content remains king!

"Under–30" Staffers at Fawcett McDermott

27

The West Coast Ad Men

H.R. Bob Haldeman, President
J. Walter Thompson
Los Angeles, California

Jack Roberts, Co–Founder,
Carson–Roberts Advertising
Los Angeles, California

My first challenge:
Key Work Clothes
in Kansas City, Missouri

Chapter Five

Know Your Customer

"The fast-flowing penetration of the internet into all households, and recently all pockets via a phone, has put an end to the domination of the mass audience. Most of the time, for most creations, it's a world of niche fulfillment."

—Kevin Kelly
The Inevitable

My new job as the Worldwide Advertising Director for the H.D. Lee Company was my first grown-up job. Until then, everyday had been a creative adventure of finding memorable ways to tell stories about our client's products or services. It had been fun.

Now, at the ripe old age of twenty-five, I had been thrust into the corporate world of managing departments, budgets, and expectations. Prior to this point in my career, I hadn't seen an invoice, much less been asked to approve one.

Chilly Welcome

My first challenge was to gain the respect and support of the seven members of my staff. I was, by far, the youngest person in the department and was replacing a gentleman who could have been a model in the famous Arrow Shirt print ads. He had been revered by the staff and retired after decades with the H.D. Lee Company.

The second-youngest person in the department was a junior media analyst turning thirty. My assistant advertising manager, who had children almost my age, was forty-one. I knew I wasn't going to be able to charm my way into their hearts. I was going to have to earn their respect through my actions. The truth was I really didn't know what I was supposed to do in my new role.

Say Hello to Corporate Politics

Prior to my appointment, the company had been acquired by the VF Corporation, which had built an immensely profitable business in women's lingerie under the Vanity Fair brand. The acquisition was not greeted with open arms by most of the existing managers. My new challenge was trying to find my place and define my role in this newly evolving environment of corporate politics at Lee.

> I knew I wasn't going to be able to charm my way into their hearts. I was going to have to earn their respect through my actions.

H.D. Lee was a $250 million a year business built on a solid foundation in the work and western wear businesses. Their products were sold through tens of thousands of specialty stores. At the time of the acquisition, the VF Corporation had collective sales of just over $40 million with almost exclusive distribution through major department stores. It was a cultural train wreck waiting to happen.

The first area our new corporate parent decided to meddle in was advertising. The H.D. Lee Company had enjoyed a long, successful relationship with Grey Advertising, a quality firm who built its reputation on New York's Seventh Avenue and understood the apparel business from the ground up.

This relationship didn't matter to the chairman of the VF Corporation. M.O. "Whitey" Lee had enjoyed a close, personal relationship with the Vanity Fair account team at a mid–sized, New York based agency named Reach McClinton Advertising. Lee was set on consolidating his advertising clout at one agency.

Around this same time, Reach McClinton, which was teetering on the brink of bankruptcy due to a combination of major account losses and general mismanagement, was acquired by the Omaha based agency, Bozell & Jacobs.

Chuck Pebbler, the president of Bozell & Jacobs, rewarded the VF Corporation for its loyalty by keeping its New York account team in place after the acquisition.

Satisfied with the resulting outcome, Lee had his corporate communication director conduct an agency review. The results were never in doubt. The New York office of Bozell & Jacobs was awarded the advertising account for the larger new fashion segment of the business, which was intended to help transition distribution for Lee into the first floor menswear departments of the major department stores. The Omaha office was assigned the major work and western product lines with a much reduced budget.

The corporate communications director was not aware of our growing business in Europe and overlooked our agency relationship there with BBDO (Batten, Barton, Durstine & Osborn).

Misguided Creative

Bozell & Jacobs had won the agency review for the new fashion product line with an ill-conceived creative concept. Models were photographed in the wild wearing a lion's head. The "Lee Lion" tagline was a focus of ridicule by our sales force and retail partners.

My first mission was to decapitate the lion. *Which I did.* This independent action did not appeal to the corporate communications director, who had been attempting to leverage his title with the agency. He lost this round and it was the last time I heard from him.

Surprisingly, this unintended power play elevated my status within my department. The company wanted a champion for our long history and industry reputation.

We settled to make the best of our relationship with our new advertising agency partner. The agency and our new account team did have an excellent grasp on developing advertising strategies and campaigns to support distribution within the major department stores. Unfortunately, we didn't have distribution to support that effort.

In the early seventies, all menswear was sold during the months of June (Father's Day), August, September (back-to-school), and December (Christmas).

The agency's recommended strategy was to create blockbuster print advertising flights during these key months and then try to leverage these efforts into expanded distribution and advance sales. While the ad campaign was having limited success with some major department store buyers, the real action and sales growth was taking place with a growing number of jeans store chains and the youth departments in those same department stores.

Unfortunately, these fashion print advertising efforts in publications such as *Playboy*, *Esquire*, *Gentleman's Quarterly*, the *New Yorker*, and the *New York Times Menswear Magazine* weren't reaching this new generation of consumers.

I had this discussion with Richard Parker, the new head of the account team at Bozell & Jacobs.

Fish Where the Fish Are

Richard Parker had built a successful career at textile industry giant, J.P. Stevens, creating non-traditional promotions with major department store chains and the movie industry. He encouraged me to think outside of the box and fish where the fish are.

Sex, Jeans, and Rock 'n' Roll

The year was 1971 and it was the golden era of rock 'n' roll. Woodstock had spawned an increasing number of music festivals around the world. Rock concert tours were being sold out with record attendance and ticket prices. The question was how could we leverage this new music popularity and fuel jean sales?

> Models were photographed in the wild wearing a lion's head. The "Lee Lion" tagline was a focus of ridicule by our sales force and retail partners. My first mission was to decapitate the lion. *Which I did.*

Mr. Parker and I strategized we could create a rock concert series to kick off during the summer shoulder period and lengthen the key back-to-school selling season. The big question was how I could get the conservative management at Lee to embrace such a non-traditional idea.

A new apparel wunderkind had recently been plucked out of VF Corporation management and named executive vice president of the H.D. Lee Company. With James Bond-type good looks, Ray Williams was a no-nonsense manager who inspired loyalty and calculated risk taking. He brought a new, can-do attitude to the company.

Baiting the Hook

With unabashed, youthful confidence, I invited Ray Williams and his wife to attend a Jethro Tull concert at the Municipal Auditorium in downtown Kansas City. To my surprise, he accepted. We had floor seats for the concert. As we entered the arena, Mr. Williams stopped, looked around, and said, "Look at all of those jeans. These are our customers!" My initial sales job was over. Now, we just had to figure out how to pull it off and fund it.

I contacted Paul Peterson, a college fraternity brother and a concert promoter for a company called Good Karma. He estimated if Lee would underwrite the series, he could pull together, stage, and produce an eight-week concert series that would be "taped live" at their new Cowtown Ballroom Venue. Unfortunately, the estimates for the series far exceeded my budget.

Sharing the Tab

Richard Parker had the answer to the funding problem. A relatively new commodity marketing cooperative,

Cotton Inc., was flush with promotional cash being fueled by the growing popularity of jeans and their natural fibers. We pitched the idea to Gary Kelly, who was the head of menswear. He embraced the idea and became our number one missionary. With Mr. Parker and Mr. Kelly's collective efforts, we were able to convince the Cotton Inc. management to split the promotional costs. The new concert series promotion would be called:

Lee & Cotton, Livin' Rock.

It was my good fortune that the agency for Cotton, Inc. was Ogilvy & Mather. It was my first introduction to this iconic, world famous agency and some of its key executives. They would end up playing a key role in my career.

> I invited Ray Williams and his wife to attend a Jethro Tull concert... ... [He] stopped, looked around, and said, "Look at all of those jeans. These are our customers!"

At the time, Levi Strauss & Co. had sales of approximately $300 million annually. Lee was their closest rival with annual sales approaching $250 million. We figured if we could leverage the strength of this summer long promotion with the major chains and department stores, we could gain significant market share during this important selling season.

Good Karma put together a stellar concert lineup including such headliners as Arlo Guthrie, Brewer & Shipley, Hall & Oates, and Linda Rondstadt. For a couple of the concerts, the opening act was Steve Martin with his famous "nose-on-the-microphone" and "arrow-thru-the-head" comedy routines.

Right Media for the Message

To further leverage our limited budget, Richard Parker and his media team at Bozell & Jacobs came up with a brilliant idea. Instead of buying the media time in key markets, they would syndicate the eight–week series in over a hundred markets on an emerging new media called FM radio. The proposal to the stations was simple.

Lee would receive a weekly, hour–long time slot between nine and ten each Saturday night during the months of June and July, along with eight minutes of advertising during each show. The radio station would retain the balance of the advertising inventory to sell.

The real incentive for the radio stations was, that by utilizing the H.D. Lee Advertising Co–op Program, that inventory was already pre–sold to area retailers.

Integrating and Involving Retailers

Local radio stations had to contribute a summer–long promotion with local retailers to drive listeners to retail locations and register for weekly drawings of Lee apparel prizes. Customers also had a chance to win an all–expense paid trip for two to London to see a live concert by The Who at White Stadium.

Mr. Parker developed incentive promotions to reward retailers for advertising, window displays, and in–store support. A similar program was designed for the Lee sales team.

The result was that H.D. Lee Company had its strongest summer selling season to date. We carved out significant market share gains with the major chains. And, we expanded our relationship with Cotton, Inc.

Why This Applies Today

In today's segmented digital world, it is even more important to understand what motivates your prospective customers, like we were able to achieve with this Lee Jeans campaign.

While the global interconnections have created the largest mass audience ever, you cannot rely only on broad-based gender profiles or demographics to reach your target.

You need to fully understand the lifestyle choices and preferences that influence your prospective customers' purchasing decisions. Make sure you are using the best targeted media vehicles to reach them.

As Kevin Kelly pointed out in his book, *The Inevitable*, "Each of these tiny niches is micro-small, but there are tens of thousands of niches."

Even though some of these niches may be relatively small, they have become increasingly easy to find via search. And, through peer based sharing, they can multiply rapidly for your specific product message.

This evolving media landscape has proven particularly challenging for the smaller advertiser to navigate as more of their advertising budgets are being allocated to digital media.

This migration is the result of the simple realization that traditional media vehicles such as newspapers and magazines became excessively expensive, and difficult to evaluate the return on investment.

Rising Importance of Mobile

If content is still king, then mobile is the emerging crown prince of media. I have often heard media executives refer to this evolution as a world that has gone from broadcast to desktop to mobile. I think that it is probably more accurate to describe this transition as a move from channels to websites to apps.

When someone conducts a search on their desktop, they tend to be researching information related to a future purchasing decision or doing a simple price comparison. When someone conducts a search on a mobile device, they are typically searching for a shopping destination and typically make a purchasing decision within ninety minutes of the search. The results are measurable, and the impact immediate.

> In today's segmented digital world, it is even more important to understand what motivates your prospective customers...

In the past, an advertisement in *Time Magazine* or a thirty second commercial in an NFL network program were big ticket items only giant firms could afford. Advertisers knew what they were buying and could negotiate a set price or contract rate.

In this new digital media world, clarity has become fragmented by the proliferation of hundreds of thousands of sites and channel options. Technology platforms have done a brilliant job of persuading smaller companies to spend money targeting these customers. Today, Facebook alone has over six million advertisers, equivalent to a fifth of all American small business firms.

Programmatic Media Buying

I am not generally a fan of programmatic media buying. My preference is usually to work more directly with a site publisher to guarantee my advertising appears in the most appropriate environment for my message and targeted customer base.

That said, this automation of the media buying and selling process has created a more efficient marketplace. The use of these sophisticated algorithms has leveled the playing field for purchasers of digital media space. Under this system, the premium space that used to be reserved for the biggest and most powerful clients or agency buying groups (much like the television sponsorship or magazine back cover) are now available in the same media bucket as the providers of plain vanilla content. My biggest concern with this rising practice is the pricing integrity and transparency in the process, which most of the large media buying groups are addressing.

But, these sophisticated media buying tools and the availability of ad metrics that are at our collective fingertips can't resolve every marketing problem or address each opportunity.

Activate the Promotion Locally

It is important to listen to your customers, involve your traditional *brick-and-mortar* or online retail partners into your programs. You should integrate them and your media partners into the strategic planning and most importantly, take the time to make sure that you know where to drop your fishing line in this expanding digital ocean.

Example of ad change progression for Lee

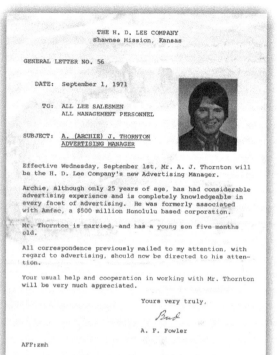

Chuck Pebbler, President
Bozell & Jacobs Advertising
Omaha, Nebraska

Richard "Dick" Parker
New head of Lee account team
Bozell & Jacobs Advertising
New York

Above: Men behind the scenes at Lee

Storyboard for a
co—op TV commercial
aired during NCAA
Football games.

Chapter Six

Disrupting Your Business Model

"Above all, our advertising executives must have the trust of independent entrepreneurs. This is not a job for lazy, frightened mediocrities."

—David Ogilvy
Principles of Management

I was busy reading my press clippings and basking in the glory of my successful Lee & Cotton campaign. It was heady stuff for a young man.

So, when Gary Kelly, my new marketing partner at Cotton, Inc. called to say he had an idea to run by me, I jumped at the chance. We scheduled a meeting for the following week during my monthly trip to New York.

Category in Transition

Gary Kelly and his team had developed a strategy for high-volume manufacturers of jeans to increase their sales and profit margins. They recognized the jean industry was going through a major transition from being just makers of durable dungarees to becoming a fashion staple for the baby-boomer generation.

> Mr. Kelly laid out his idea. It was brilliant in its simplicity. ...the prestige value of designer goods would command premium pricing.

At the time, the retail price was $11.95 for Lee Rider denim jeans. More fashionable models in corduroy, chambray, or brushed twill fabrics were going for as much as $14.95. From Lee's perspective, these premium prices were far from the commodity pricing structure of only a few years back, when work wear and western jeans were priced by the dozen at wholesale.

Challenging the Norm

Mr. Kelly laid out his idea. It was brilliant in its simplicity. Lee would approach a major luxury designer brand and partner with them to market a new designer jean. Their rationale was that the prestige value of designer goods would command premium pricing.

They estimated if we designed a fashion jean model out of a lighter denim weight, like the ten–ounce jeans marketed exclusively to women, we could wholesale the product for $18 to $20. Even with a licensing fee of 6 to 8 percent to our designer brand partner, the arithmetic was straightforward. We could nearly triple our wholesale selling price and the retailer would benefit as well.

Testing the Waters

Given the VF Corporations mandate that we increase distribution in the main floor menswear departments of the major department stores, I felt this upscale strategy would be welcomed with open arms.

We scheduled a meeting with the senior merchandising executives at Lee to lay out the strategy, complete with design ideas, trade marketing materials, and retailer promotional concepts.

Not our Style

To say that we were laughed out of the room would be an understatement. They lambasted us with reasons why our idea wouldn't benefit the company.

While some felt this kind of effort would divert our attention from growing the Lee Brand, the underlying reason seemed to be the executives were convinced there was not a market for forty dollar jeans.

No Prophet is Accepted in His Own Land

Six months later, Bloomingdale's Department Store in New York launched a new line of designer jeans called the "Cigarette Jean." It was available only in a slim, straight leg model of double–dyed, ten–ounce denim with a pack of cigarettes in the hip pocket. The retail price was forty dollars. This new product introduction turned the industry on its head.

> …the executives were convinced there was not a market for forty dollar jeans. …Six months later, Bloomingdale's launched a new line of designer jeans… The retail price was forty dollars.

A few months later, an importer leveraged the Gloria Vanderbilt name to launch another successful version of the designer jean. I went back to focusing on my advertising responsibilities. Later that year, I was tapped to head our new men's and women's top division for North America and Europe.

There are No Bad Ideas

The failed new product effort taught me one of the most important lessons I would learn during my career. At the same time, my hard work resulted in a promotion that introduced me to the world of product management, financial planning, and profit and loss responsibility.

I learned an advertisement isn't always the solution to a marketing problem or opportunity. Often, it is the ability to recognize issues or opportunities that can exist by revising the current packaging or product design, addressing competitive pricing strategies, or identifying areas for market expansion.

MEN'S WEAR

Smith   Thornton   Waller   Niswonger

THE LEE MEN:
Geniuses With Jeans

What is a designer? Is it someone who simply originates fashion ideas? Or does he fit the traditional image of a sartorial sophisticate busily sketching, scouring the market for fabrics and then draping his creation.

Unfortunately, in the men's industry there is no clear-cut definition of what constitutes a designer. Few operations employ stylists who fit the traditional mold. However, in most large corporate structures, the design function is found in the merchandising arm. Such is the case with the H.D. Lee Co., where merchandisers, who do not claim to be innovators, are creators of the jeans-oriented line. Their concepts, universally popular with both the chic and non-chic, represent the acme of fashion today. And, if they refuse to be called designers, they must admit to being creative merchandisers.

SHAWNEE MISSION, Kan.—At H.D. Lee Co., one of the country's top three jeans producers, they play the fashion game for big stakes. So, when John Waller, fashion division merchandise manager and his team work on a new line, they aren't out "just to design pretty products." Instead, they consider two basic but key criteria—Can the item be produced? Secondly, does it have mass appeal?

The team has apparently scored well in answering both questions. Although the firm does not provide volume figures by division, fashion is the fastest growing sector, attests William J. McKenna, president of Lee. (A division of VF Corp., Lee's total volume last year climbed 23.1 per cent to $190,562,000.)

Yet, it is the 86-year-old firm's ability to design for a wide range of consumers that has catapulted it to the forefront of fashion leadership. "If you're going to mass produce fashion, it has to be relatively safe or the mass market won't adopt it," Waller asserts.

The team's interpretation of the mass fashion appetite has been more than adequate. It has helped propel the Lee line to a popularity and identification on the international level that is equal to Levi's and Wrangler.

To maintain their awareness of what the consumer wants, Waller's staff keeps a close eye on the street scene and receives feedback from retailers and Lee's own sales representatives. In addition, they attend trade shows abroad twice each year. While visiting cities such as London, Rome, Paris and Copenhagen, Waller relates, they also study clothes being worn by Europeans. The staff also shops the fabric market five or six times a year.

THE FASHION TEAM

Designated merchandise managers, the fashion team is comprised of 33-year-old Jim Niswonger, who is responsible for woven slacks, jeans and coordinate tops; Len Smith, 37, the knit slacks, jeans and coordinate tops merchandiser; and 27-year-old Archie Thornton, who

heads the shirt area.

Shirts are the newest addition to the fashion division. "Last September was the first selection of shirts we could call a line. It's a collection of shirts to go with jeans," Waller explains. In addition to shirts in the fashion division, Thornton is shirt merchandiser for Lee's Western and Ms. Lee divisions.

Impeccably dressed, Waller at 46, provides leadership for the team which also includes Ulf Lundqvist, a Swedish-born, New York-based stylist. Employed full-time by the company, Lundqvist works closely with the fashion staff. "Ulf's influence is very strong on the line," Waller comments, and the merchandisers credit him with an amazing ability to interpret what is happening in America and its impact on fashion.

The team begins developing a new line 31 weeks prior to its release to salesmen, Waller points out. "The only thing that takes place beforehand is some yarn and color development for knits." (Lee employs a substantial share of the

Disrupt or Die

The typical life span for the average Fortune 500 company is rarely over thirty years. The reasons are many and varied. Some products and services are leapfrogged by technological advances, while some companies are mismanaged and ultimately go out of business. Other companies are acquired by better managed, faster growing competitors. But, for the most part, it is part of the normal growth cycle for a business.

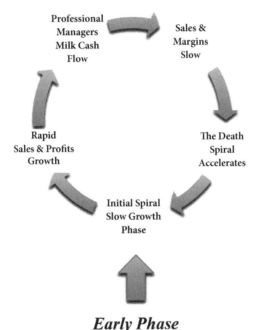

Early Phase
During the first few years of a typical business, the growth is slow & managed by its founders.

Management Transition
In this phase of the growth cycle, Professional Managers are hired to deliver better financial results.

Professional Managers Milk Cash Flow

Sales & Margins Slow

The Death Spiral Accelerates

The Growth Years
In Phase Two of its business cycle, the company's growth & profits accelerate.

Rapid Sales & Profits Growth

Initial Slow Growth Phase

Reinvent & Disrupt

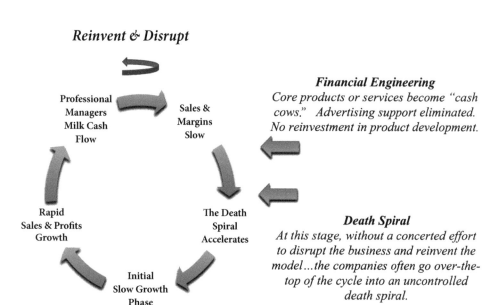

Professional Managers Milk Cash Flow

Sales & Margins Slow

Rapid Sales & Profits Growth

The Death Spiral Accelerates

Initial Slow Growth Phase

Financial Engineering
Core products or services become "cash cows." Advertising support eliminated. No reinvestment in product development.

Death Spiral
At this stage, without a concerted effort to disrupt the business and reinvent the model…the companies often go over-the-top of the cycle into an uncontrolled death spiral.

Change was Encouraged

After I joined Ogilvy & Mather, I found out all account managers were encouraged to go to their clients, once or twice a year, with non-advertising or promotional ideas to help their clients profitably grow their businesses.

We weren't restricted to the type of recommendations. It could be related to a product line extension opportunity, a new product feature, a packaging concept, or a strategic partnership opportunity.

An example of such an outside-the-box idea is one that I proposed to the Hershey's Chocolate account management team at Ogilvy & Mather in 1983. It was to consider teaming up with Hawaii based Mauna Loa Macadamia Nut company to create the "Great Hawaiian Hershey Bar." The account team loved the idea and presented it to Hershey's marketing management. As you can read from the newspaper clipping, Hershey finally recognized the potential in this idea when they purchased Mauna Loa twenty-one years later.

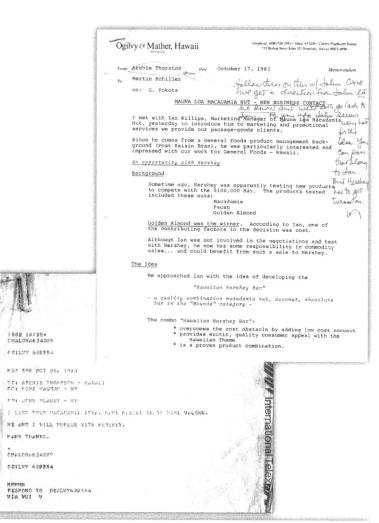

Chapter Seven

Sell or Else

"…set yourself to becoming the best-informed person in the agency on the account to which you have been assigned."

—David Ogilvy
Confessions of an Advertising Man

David Ogilvy recognized early in his advertising career if you were going to be a successful agency, it was your job to create great advertising that moved products off the shelf. The mantra, **We Sell or Else!** became the Ogilvy & Mather slogan.

Ultimate responsibility was constantly reinforced throughout the company's far–flung network of offices in countless training sessions, company publications, newsletters, and films (referred to as "Magic Lanterns" by Mr. Ogilvy).

Often, this message was conveyed through case studies that chronicled the success of client campaigns. Like the memorable campaign for American Express: "Don't Leave Home Without it!" Or the iconic tagline for General Food's Maxwell House Coffee brand which promised it was "Good to the Last Drop!" Or the legendary campaign for Dove Soap, which touted that each bar contained "Twenty–five Percent Cleansing Cream!"

This advertising claim helped propel the brand to a profit in its first year—a rare feat in the marketing world then.

> I never had a client wake up in the morning and say, "Today, what I want to do is buy an ad."

David Ogilvy believed outstanding advertising needed to be original in concept and execution to produce exceptional results and drive sales. He said, "We will rarely create big ideas by always playing it safe!"

Prior to joining Ogilvy & Mather, I had the privilege to work on two product introductions that reinforced this concept.

Happy Meal

The Happy Meal was not developed or designed to be a new menu board item for the McDonald's chain. Then, like now, McDonald's had seasonal promotional themes to help endorse various business segments.

One perplexing promotional vertical was dubbed Family Dinner. At the time, the evening meal day–part was the weakest business segment for the chain. McDonald's reasoned that, if they could position their restaurants as an affordable alternative for family dining, they could improve profitability for their franchisees and company–owned stores.

From company research, we knew parents of small children never ordered a complete meal for the child. Typically, the parents would order either a small hamburger or small fries with a small drink that they would often share with the child.

Also, parents found it difficult to enjoy their own meal when the children were running around the restaurant.

Bob Bernstein, founder and president of Bernstein-Rein Advertising, reckoned both problems could be resolved by introducing a new promotional item—the Happy Meal.

His original concept was to package a complete children's meal including a hamburger or cheeseburger with a small fries and soft drink.

The meal would come packaged in a promotional container that was designed to occupy the child's attention. To make it even more attractive to children, a premium item was included in the package.

The eight-week promotional campaign kicked off in eight Midwest, Rocky Mountain, and Desert Southwest market locations. By the third week, the franchisees were clamoring for additional Happy Meal packaging. By year-end, it was made a menu board item and has become an iconic staple for the chain.

This was not my idea, but I did have the privilege of working with the account management team at Bernstein-Rein on the development of the Happy Meal concept. My role included supervising the original price elasticity study, working with the agency production department to design and fabricate the prototype packaging, and authoring the ordering guidelines for the promotional Blue Book.

Lee Riders Boy's Wear

A promotional concept for Lee Rider boy's division was developed to support the expanded production capacity H.D. Lee had financed to broaden the customer base for our expanding line of jean products.

Our sales and marketing team interviewed countless retailers of boy's wear, in addition to conducting numerous focus groups of mothers. But, the real breakthrough came when the Omaha office of Bozell & Jacobs did a series of one-on-one interviews with actual users of the products.

A promotion rolled out in eight Midwestern test markets during the summer of 1972 that offered free iron-on back patches with every jean jacket purchased. The promotion had to be pulled after just four weeks when consumer demand out-stripped production capacity.

An integral part contributing to the success of this promotion was a promotional flyer that the sales force used to sell-in the promotion. The entire package included in-store posters, co-op ad slicks, window design ideas, and iron-on back patches.

The television campaign that launched in 1972 to support the promotion is timeless, and would still move the sales needle for retailers today. Big ideas are based on original concepts that were relevant then, and would remain relevant today.

At Ogilvy & Mather, I never had a client wake up in the morning and say, "Today, what I want to do is buy an ad."

Later in my career, when I was running the travel group for Ogilvy & Mather, I recognized what really motivated my clients was putting heads-in-beds and butts-in-seats.

Throughout my career, I tried to drive a simple fact home to my account teams. When meeting with or talking to the client, I recommended to always focus on what was important to that client, whether it be advance bookings, profit margins, or competitive pressures. Rarely, if ever, was a new advertisement important unless designed to resolve one of those specific problems.

> Big ideas are based on original concepts that were relevant then, and would remain relevant today.

What Moves the Sales Needle?

To become a truly successful advertising or marketing executive and be conversant in the business, you must become a student of your client or company's distribution channels. It is here you can discover the key issues that can derail or support any advertising or promotional campaign.

Any marketing success is dependent on a thorough understanding of how these distribution channels function. You need to be sure that you have all the necessary programs in place to support these channels when you launch any new advertising or promotional effort.

Each industry has developed its own, unique distribution systems and channel partners. I have always encouraged my account management teams to invest their time to fully understand each industry's challenges.

There are several ways to learn about your client's business. These can include, but are not limited to: making sales calls with field sales personnel, visiting with buyers and marketing personnel of major retailers or marketing partners, attending trade shows, conducting retail or online "secret shopper" surveys, and most importantly, buying and using their product or service, whether from a traditional brick–and–mortar location or online.

In *Confessions of an Advertising Man*, David Ogilvy wrote how to become the most informed person in the agency:

"If it is a gasoline account, read text books on the chemistry, geology and distribution of petroleum products. Read all of the trade journals in the field. Read all of the research reports and marketing plans that your agency has ever written on the product.

Spend Saturday mornings in service stations pumping gas and talking to motorists. Visit your client's refineries and research laboratories. Study the advertising of their competitors. At the end of the year, you will know more about gasoline than your boss!"

Left to right, top row:
The Original Happy Meal Blue Book;
The Original Happy Meal prototype;

Left to right, bottom row:
Front Flyer for the retail sales
materials package for Lee Riders
promotion which included Back Patches;
Story board for Original TV advertisement

Chapter Eight

Business Writing Secrets

"You don't need a special gift for writing to develop the ability to write effectively. The process of writing is hard work, even for the best writers. But, the principles of good writing are simple, easy to understand and easy to put to work."

—Ken Roman
Writing that Works

It had only been a year since I had been recruited to help open the new Ogilvy & Mather Honolulu office.

Servicing Big Clients

The primary reason for the expansion was to service the new General Foods Asia/Pacific headquarters. General Foods had decided to open a facility in Honolulu for pure logistic reasons. At the time, airlines could not fly non–stop from the US mainland to Asia and were required to stop in Honolulu to refuel. An additional benefit was management could speak with their headquarters in White Plains or Rye, New York during regular business hours in the morning; and speak with their representatives in Australia, Japan or China in the afternoon. It was a good solution.

I had been tapped to run the Asia/Pacific and World Trade Divisions of General Foods, which was an important division of the agency's largest client at the time. It was a heady time, when consumer products companies like General Foods were spending millions of dollars building and supporting such major brands as Maxwell House Coffee, Country Time Lemonade, Shake 'n' Bake, and Post Cereals.

My Ticket to the Dance

It was the summer of 1982 when I received an invitation to attend the Ogilvy & Mather *Senior Account Management Program*. This program, which was initiated by David Ogilvy himself, was core to the success of the agency. The invitees were, for the most part, managers of one of the agency's global accounts or a major regional business.

Mr. Ogilvy was a firm believer that our company training was key to our global success. He insisted this program be conducted solely by senior management: chairmen, CEOs, and presidents of our major departments. From my perspective, it was like having an oak leaf cluster pinned onto your shoulder.

Homework Assignment

As I was busy packing my obligatory red suspenders and grey flannel suits for the trip, I received an internal memo from the agency's current president, Ken Roman. He announced that he would be conducting an afternoon–long session on successful business communication and writing skills during the program.

In preparation for his session, Mr. Roman was requiring each of us to submit three writing samples prior to the program:

- A letter or memo introducing a new concept idea
- A letter intended to persuade a client or associate to support your position
- A letter defending the agency's position on a campaign

I had a few weeks to complete the submissions and I set out to dazzle the agency's president with my business acumen. I figured if I peppered my writing submissions with large amounts of General Foods data related to market share trends, brand development indexes, profit margins and sales numbers, I would impress management with my overall grasp of the client's business and reinforce my perceived value to the agency.

The results of this effort were three page rambling drafts even I found boring. I continued to try to buff the submissions until the deadline and ultimately sent them off in the agency "pouch" that provided two-day delivery service to New York.

The day of the deadline, the client had a crisis that required immediate attention. Before heading out of the office to address the problem, I dictated a cover memo to my assistant.

My hope was the sheer bulk of information shoehorned into the writing assignments would overwhelm my lack of style.

A few weeks later, I arrived in Toronto. The session on business communications and writing skills took place on the second day of the program. The sixteen members of the program were seated when Ken Roman entered the room carrying two six-inch thick briefcases.

He placed the two briefcases on the front table and began to tell us a story:

> *"Every evening, when I leave the office around 6:30 p.m., my assistant hands me these two briefcases. One contains only letters or memos addressed directly to me. The other has copies of communications I have been copied on…"*

He opened each briefcase to reveal both contained two high stacks of paper.

> *"After dinner, I pour myself a glass of scotch and retire to my home office to tackle these stacks of paper."*

Breaking Out in Cold Sweat

After allowing this scenario into our minds, he projected a letter onto a screen. It was a two–page, single–spaced letter about various points of minutia related to a current campaign. I was sitting like a deer caught in the headlights. The pages resembled my own writing samples. I was convinced I would be on the next non–stop flight back to Honolulu.

Then, in a side–by–side comparison, he projected another writing sample onto the screen. To my amazement, it was the hastily written cover memo that accompanied my writing samples. Roman continued:

> *"When you look at this volume of information that I have to address every evening, which author do you think has a better chance of being promoted in my mind?"*

This real world example got all our attention. Then, the real learning began.

I am not going to attempt to provide you with a step–by–step recap of the real–life lessons and examples that Ken

Roman shared with us during that particular afternoon session. Instead, I am going to give you my takeaway of the session: what I learned, how it helped me advance my career, and how those lessons still apply in today's digital world.

For those of you who would like a more in–depth peek into Ken Roman's lessons regarding business communications, I highly recommend *Writing that Works*, co–authored by Ken Roman and Joel Raphaelson. Raphaelson was also an Ogilvy & Mather executive. This book has valuable lessons for any executive who would like to improve communication skills.

Secret to Writing that Works

In every form of written communication, you are really writing an advertisement for yourself. What you say, the way you say it, and the form in which it is delivered, says a great deal about you and how you feel about the recipient. Like in Roman's examples, you can't bore your audience over to your side.

Digital Dangers

Today, mistakes or misstatements can last an eternity in the digital world. I have personally witnessed careers being shortened or permanently damaged from using automated writing aids or shortcuts.

I highly recommend you exercise extreme caution when employing potentially dangerous writing aids such as:

Reply All—Think twice before broadcasting a reply and make sure that you select the right audience for your message.
Spell Check or Auto Correct—Not only can these aids dramatically alter the meaning of your message, they imply that you are sloppy. Edit, edit, and re–edit.

Social Media Posting—Pictures or opinions posted on sites may seem humorous to close friends but have the potential to damage careers.

Get to the Point

Similar to Ken Roman's example, everyone is overwhelmed by the volume of messages received daily, whether by email, text, or chat. Here are my six points to address the crucial issues that we face to get our writing noticed, understood, and acted upon:

1. *Keep it Short and to the Point*

   Determine what you want the recipient to remember, even if they don't read your entire message.

2. *Highlight What You Want Remembered*

   Put the key topic of the email in a bold face, centered headline.

   Use bold face subheads to separate your writing to create a memorable message.

3. *Put Emphasis on Key Supporting Points*

   Don't be afraid to <u>underscore</u> or use *italics* to put an emphasis on key supporting facts within your messages.

4. *Separate the Call-to-Action*

   I have found it helps to separate the call-to-action or recap of your message from the body of the email, text, letter or memo so it is not overlooked, such as a centered line or series of asterisks.

5. *Make the Recipient Feel Important*

Always use appropriate salutations. You want to let the recipient know that they are important to you.

6. *Think Before Hitting the Send Button*

David Ogilvy was convinced that successful writing was the result of editing. Edit, review again, then hit send.

Right:
Dress up emails with formatting. Use bullet lists, bold, italics and underlining for emphasis. And don't forget to edit, edit, edit....

Left:
Cover Letter writing sample

Get this book!

I graduated.

Chapter Nine

Brand Secrets Revealed

"We must make advertising that sells, but first, make advertising that builds brands."

—David Ogilvy
The Business of Big Ideas

How I Learned the Meaning of a Brand

While I had been in the advertising business for over a decade, I had a very limited understanding of the term.

My enlightenment process began to take place in 1982. I had moved to the new Ogilvy & Mather Hawaii office in 1981 to manage the General Foods Asia/Pacific and World Trade accounts. Our solid consumer packaged goods discipline proved to be the perfect foundation to attract the regional advertising accounts of other major consumer product companies.

One of our first major wins was the Coca Cola Bottling Company of Hawaii. Our day-to-day contact on the Islands was Roger Morey, a solid beverage marketing professional.

Through our promotional work helping Coca Cola prepare for the 1984 Summer Olympics in Los Angeles, California, I met Tom Kemp, the chairman and CEO of the

Coca Cola Bottling Company of Los Angeles, a beverage behemoth that controlled most of the company's retail bottling business west of the Mississippi.

It was through both Mr. Morey and Tom Kemp that I became involved with the US Olympic Committee and helped found the Friends of the US Olympic Committee in Hawaii. Tom Kemp and I developed a lifelong friendship, a nice bonus.

The Era of the Pepsi Challenge

The Coca Cola Company's market share lead over its chief competitor, Pepsi Cola, had been slowly slipping for nearly fifteen consecutive years. Most of us close to the business attributed this decline to Pepsi's aggressive Pepsi Challenge advertising campaign. Through its consumer taste studies, Pepsi had been able to determine in blind taste tests, Pepsi was preferred over Coca Cola by many population groups.

Most beverage insiders knew this preference was due to Pepsi's brix level (the sugar content of a beverage) which left consumers with a sweeter, more pleasant aftertaste than Coca Cola.

> The Brand is simply a relationship between a product or service and its customer.

In a category-wide blind taste test, the hands–down winner was always Royal Crown Cola. But, in the head–to–head competition between the category leaders, this fact was always overlooked.

So, after exhaustive blind taste tests with hundreds of thousands of participants, Coca Cola decided to abandon their fabled secret formula and adopt the new formula preferred in the test.

Consumer Outcry

While this new formula scored well in blind taste tests, what company executives didn't consider when launching "New Coke" was the special relationship Coca Cola had with its customers. **The brand is simply a relationship between a product or service and its customer.**

Coca Cola: The Product

Coca Cola, the product, is a combination of several things: an aluminum can with red and white ink, fructose, water with CO_2, caramel coloring, and syrup based flavoring.

> The consumer relationship with the product is the foundation of a brand.

Coca Cola: The Brand

The brand (or relationship) is something much different. It's the memory of a Fourth of July family picnic, your first movie date, or a baseball doubleheader with your dad. **The consumer relationship with the product is the foundation of a brand.** Ultimately, people didn't want the management of Coca Cola fooling around with their relationship to the brand.

The Consumer Wins

After seventy–nine days of fielding an ever–increasing barrage of consumer criticisms and complaints, Coca Cola executives relented and announced the return of the original formula—now called Coca Cola Classic.

Today, after a renewed focus on the relationship and how it is impacted by beverage preference trends, Coca Cola remains the fourth most valuable brand in the world. This is a testament to the strength of that relationship—the strength of the brand.

> I have always held the strong belief that advertising and marketing people are the true builders and stewards of brands.

Traditional Understanding

In its most widely accepted definition, a brand is the trademark for a company's product or service. But, even in its most basic form, it is much more than a product name and logo. A brand represents the real underlying value of any company to its employees, current shareholders, or future owners. This essence of a brand and its marketplace value is carried on a company's balance sheet in the form of goodwill.

Anyone interested in investing in, or acquiring, a company knows that the real worth of that company lies in the value and strength of its brand(s). More modern manufacturing facilities can always be built. Employees can be replaced. Brands are hard to build and, in most cases, impossible to replicate.

A Most Misunderstood Term

A brand is not only a name, logo, package design, or slogan. Over the last few years, reporters, sports commentators, and celebrity talk show hosts are using the term casually (and inaccurately) to describe anything or anyone with a public presence.

During the last republican presidential primaries, I witnessed a media report on the fundraising progress of the unusually large slate of candidates. A political pundit was giving an overview of the results and the political future of the candidates.

The commentator stated the report had disclosed most of the campaign money raised to date had been used for the purchase of yard signs, buttons, bumper stickers, and caps sporting their candidate's campaign slogans, *because the voters said they wanted to be part of their candidate's brand.*

The misconception of the term "brand" is not limited to the uninformed as shown in the examples above.

I have always held the strong belief that advertising and marketing people are the true builders and stewards of brands.

Many years back, I had the occasion to meet with an executive of the Doner Advertising Firm in Irvine, California about a possible promotional opportunity for their Mazda automobile account.

One of my goals during the meeting was to better understand how this promotional program might help to strengthen work for Mazda and increase vehicle sales.

I asked the senior account manager how he would describe the Mazda brand. He put his feet up on the desk, leaned back and said, "Zoom–Zoom!" I thanked him for his time and left the building.

What I had expected him to elaborate on was how the performance aspects of their unique engine and drive train gave their buyers a sporty feel of exhilaration for a mid-priced line of compact sedans and coupes. With the agency's focus on the importance of a tagline over its relationship with its customer, it did not surprise me to learn that they had lost this major account a few years later.

Relationship Relevance Today

In today's ever-changing and evolving world of technology, it is important to understand how to build and nurture a relationship between your product or service. The customer is more important than ever.

Your Brand and Bond

Your brand and bond ultimately helps:
- Cement customer loyalty
- Defend against app or product churn
- Encourage a customer to overlook or forgive a system outage
- Provide customers with the patience to work through a system upgrade that creates more problems than it was designed to fix.

Making it Work

Today, Apple is one of the world's most valued brands. Apple has not been created by any notable advertising effort or creative execution though. In fact, for a company of its size and valuation, Apple invests relatively little in traditional brand advertising.

What Apple does do, however, is focus its entire company effort on maintaining and nurturing its relationship with its loyal customer base.

Apple established the foundation for this relationship early in its history by introducing easy-to-use tools that empowered the individual to achieve their goals—at the work place or in their everyday life. Then, they packaged these game-changing tools in revolutionary designs which didn't conform to the accepted, traditional industry standards.

Their approach enabled the user to wear the iMac, iPod, or iPhone as a validation of their personal embrace of technology advancements, much like someone can *wear* brands such as Chivas scotch as a symbol of their sophistication or BMW as a demonstration of their search for performance.

Apple continuously strives to reinforce this relationship by introducing innovative new technology tools and designs for categories that build on this simple mission.

Whether revolutionizing the music industry, reinventing the mobile phone experience, introducing a new wearable category, or addressing the future of entertainment in the home, Apple understands the value of its brand and the importance of relationships.

By focusing on this mission, Apple has created product continuity from which the brand builds upon its existing foundation and customer relationships to ensure future growth in sales and company valuation.

Roger Morey
Marketing;
Coca Cola Bottling Company,
Hawaii

Thomas P. Kemp
Chairman & CEO;
Coca Cola Bottling Company,
Los Angeles

Tom Kemp introducing the Summer Olympics
Mascot

Chapter Ten

Rewards of Risk Taking

"A ship is always safe at the shore—but that is not what it is built for."

—Albert Einstein

Any large, multinational advertising account such as General Foods Asia/Pacific and World Trade has less glamorous operating components. In this case, it was the food service division of the business that served the Alaska, Hawaii, Guam and American Samoa markets.

General Foods had a small annual budget and most of the work consisted of business–to–business print advertisements in trade magazines throughout the region or small print runs of point–of–sale materials, such as table tents, menu promotions, or incentive programs for the sales teams.

The redeeming quality was the client, Ross Jasper, a hardworking professional with a real creative side to his management style.

The food service division had an extensive product offering ranging from brands like Country Time Lemonade, Jell–O, and Post Cereals for the mom 'n' pop diners, and Open Pit Barbecue Sauce for some of the nationally recognized barbecue chains.

The bulk of their sales volume was generated by the company's major coffee brands of Maxwell House, Sanka, and Yuban.

Within the visitor destination markets of Hawaii and Guam, the importance of the coffee business translated into regular, daily deliveries by the container load. It was a lucrative, high volume business, but the commodity pricing nature of coffee made it a very competitive category that the hotel and resort food service buyers were always quick to exploit.

Trouble Brewing on the Horizon

In Hawaii, some local roasters were making inroads with the upscale hotels and resorts by marketing coffee made from Kona coffee beans grown on the Big Island of Hawaii. While a pure, 100% Kona coffee left a slightly bitter aftertaste, the tropical positioning and allure was proving to be a successful selling point to the hotel's food and beverage operations and their guests.

> If you want to succeed in business, you must be willing to take certain risks.

During Ronald Reagan's first term in the White House and in an effort to promote Made-in-America products, President Regan had the White House Chef introduce Kona Coffee to the daily menu. Mr. Ross recognized the sales potential for General Foods.

But, Kona coffee did have its down sides. First, was the finish, and second, it was expensive, given the small number of growers and the limited size of the annual Kona crop.

Leverage Your Size

Mr. Ross's creative solution to these issues was to leverage General Foods' buying power in the category. His idea was to create a coffee product that blended a smaller percentage of the rich, but somewhat harsh, Kona bean with a milder Columbia-grown bean, similar to those used in the premium Yuban coffee brand. The result was a rich, aromatic Island coffee with a smoother flavor.

Ross had always been a team player and had worked closely with Ogilvy during the development process. I was convinced Mr. Ross had a winner on his hands. Then, the not-created-here-in-White Plains issue raised its ugly head.

All General Foods coffee products considered for development automatically fell under its industry leading behemoth, Maxwell House Coffee Division.

Not Created Here

The division had some of the industry's leading experts in product sourcing, roasting, innovation and marketing. But, similar to any bureaucracy, they had a tendency to protect their turf.

Mr. Ross presented the opportunity and his plan for implementation on several occasions. The result was always the same. The Kona product wasn't right for General Foods because the availability of coffee beans was unreliable. The commodity pricing for the beans didn't reflect the overall market pricing. The initial market was too small and speculative to divert roasting and packaging resources.

I felt maybe the idea wasn't getting a fair hearing because it hadn't been conceived in White Plains and therefore didn't have a supportive missionary at the headquarters.

In regards to working with an account the size of General Foods, it wasn't generally considered a wise career move to go around the management teams of one of your largest advertisers. This was particularly true if you were in a remote branch office working on a regional part of a major client's business.

But, during my years at Ogilvy, I had come to realize the employees truly practiced what they preached. One of the guiding principles at Ogilvy & Mather was, *One Agency -Indivisible*. If you had a problem with a creative project, media implementation, or promotional opportunity, the other offices were always there to help. They never asked what was in it for them from a revenue standpoint. They just asked what you needed and then did it.

I didn't really want to engage the team that handled the Maxwell House brand or the management for the entire account since it could create unnecessary tension in their day-to-day business dealings with the client.

Evoking Higher Powers

I decided to take the problem to a higher level. I wrote a brief memo outlining the opportunity and the current roadblock to Ken Roman, the Ogilvy & Mather president. I asked Mr. Roman if he would be comfortable intervening on my client's behalf. His response was to get on a train to White Plains to meet with Erv Shames, the president of General Foods–USA.

Mr. Roman pleaded our case strictly based on the facts that I had outlined in the memo.

The next week, the client received a telex giving him the go-ahead on the project. The only stipulation was we would have to source the initial production quantities through a co-packer.

Over the next six months, the agency worked hand-inglove with the client to bring Horizon® Kona Blend coffee to market. The industry response was overwhelming and sales volumes exceeded projections.

The following year, Ross Jasper and his food service division received the General Foods Chairman's Award for product innovation.

> By reaching out for non–conventional help, I was able to help both my client and myself gain recognition for innovative thinking.

The Rewards of Risk Taking

If you want to succeed in business, you must be willing to take certain risks. Great businesses or business successes are not built by managing the status quo. Whether you call it "rocking the boat" or "thinking outside of the box," you must be willing to embrace change and ideas that threaten the norm.

Being an agent for change is particularly necessary in today's rapidly evolving technology businesses. If you are not willing to stir up the pot, and become one of the disrupters, your idea will likely become another road kill along the digital highway.

By reaching out for non–conventional help, I was able to help both my client and myself gain recognition for innovative thinking. It also helped there were partners at Ogilvy & Mather you could trust.

Ogilvy & Mather
Advertising

2 East 48th Street New York, New York 10017
Telephone: 1 212 907 3400 • Telex: 620554 and 12279 • Cables: Flagbearer New York

KENNETH ROMAN, JR.
President

March 14, 1984

ARCHIE THORNTON
Hawaii

Dear Arch:

You can tell Ross Jasper that I carried his case for Kona Coffee to the highest levels of General Foods this week -- to Erv Shames and Jim Whitcomb.

You can't tell him that I made the sale, but I did get Jim to question Tom Neylon about what was being done to move the project forward. Tom said that some kind of decision had to be made in the next 45 days, and that he was gathering the information.

I quoted from your letter that talked about this as a specialty product in the Pacific region. Jim had some questions about the quantity of beans which might be available under an investment plan. All that is being looked into, I understand.

Following those meetings, I went a step further and decided to slip the idea to Art Trotman, the Managing Director of Cottee's General Foods in Australia.

Let's see if anything comes out of all this.

By the way, the coffee is very good.

Yours,

KR:rjk

cc: John Blaney
      Marty Schiller

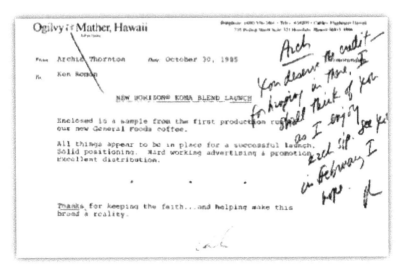

Ogilvy & Mather, Hawaii

From   Archie Thornton   Rev October 30, 1985

To   Ken Roman

NEW HORIZON® KONA BLEND LAUNCH

Enclosed is a sample from the first production run of
our new General Foods coffee.

All things appear to be in place for a successful launch.
Solid positioning. Hard working advertising & promotion.
Excellent distribution.

Thanks for keeping the faith...and helping make this
brand a reality.

[handwritten note] Arch, You deserve the credit for hanging in there. I shall think of you as I enjoy a second sip. See you in February I hope.

Hawaiian Horizon
Kona Blend Coffee
packaging

Ogilvy & Mather
Advertising

2 East 48th Street New York, New York 10017
Telephone: 1 212 907-3400 • Telex: 620554 and 12279 • Cables: Flagbearer New York

JOHN R. BLANEY
General Manager

November 9, 1983

Mr. Jeffrey Perls
General Foods International
250 North Street
White Plains, New York 10625

Dear Jeff:

This will forward an idea put forth by our office in Hawaii. It surfaced during the recent "scan" of our offices as we looked for new business ideas for General Foods International.

The opportunity is to expand your Kona-Blend Horizon coffee into retail distribution. As you know, Kona-Blend is now a food-service product.

Kona Coffee is:

.   a rich, aromatic bean
.   consistently, one of the world's highest priced beans
.   the only domestic bean being served in the White House
.   recognized and valued in the U.S.A., Canada and Japan
.   currently being produced in the San Leandro plant

By acquiring, or entering into an exclusive broker arrangement with United Coffee Corporation, GF could generate an immediate contribution to the bottom line with little or no risk...and benefit from a real, newsworthy quality/value story.

A regional specialty retail launch of this existing food-service brand, would require minimal funding while contributing significantly to GF's quality profile in the Pacific.

For your consideration.

Cordially,

John R. Blaney

JRB:cs
cc: John Cassaday   Erv Shames
    Ken Roman   Jerry Wollert
    Marty Schiller
    Archie Thornton

Many thanks, Archie

Chapter Eleven

Learning from Your Mistakes

*"You don't learn to walk by following the rules.
You learn by doing and falling over!"*

—Sir Richard Branson
Founder, Virgin Group

The year was 1993. I was on a floating lounger in my pool on the windward side of Oahu contemplating my future. I had just presided over the winding down of an ill–fated, retail concept chain I founded after leaving Ogilvy & Mather in 1987.

The concept was a good one, built on solid business planning. The visitor industry was booming and a casual apparel trend at the office was sweeping the nation.

My Big Retail Mistake

My idea was to create an upscale, men's retail chain, Kula Bay, that evoked the lifestyle and imagery of the tropics from a time gone by. It made news from the day we opened our first retail store in the small town of Lahaina on the Island of Maui.

The Retail Reporting Corporation named it *One of the Top 100 Retail Concepts* of the decade.

Opportunities to expand our retail stores into high–profile locations and resorts poured in.

The idea was simple from the onset. Open a chain of stores located in prominent visitor destinations, then use the awareness created among the visitors to expand into a larger, more lucrative wholesale business. We were just making headway in part two of the strategy, when the bottom fell out of the market.

Good Idea, Bad Timing

My big idea fell victim to the meltdown in travel—a by–product of the first Gulf War. The economic slump in California that was magnified by plummeting real estate values didn't help. The downfall may also have been compounded by management being distracted from recognizing the need for corrective action in the wake of numerous industry awards and glowing media reviews.

As I floated in my pool, I was keenly aware of other pressing issues besides my bruised ego. The retail venture had burned up the hard–earned capital I had been able to accumulate during my previous career. To further complicate my situation, I had no job or any prospects of finding one in the middle of the Pacific.

Never Burn Your Bridges

Then, the phone rang. The head of the Ogilvy & Mather office in Honolulu had used the ruse that the agency was shuttering its Hawaii operation and orchestrated a breakaway from the agency the previous night. He was opening his own firm. In a short twenty–four hour period, he had recruited the vast majority of the employees and clients to join him in this new venture.

My next call came from Graham Phillips, the former CEO of Ogilvy & Mather Worldwide, and Clif Kagawa, who ran the Hill & Knowlton operations in the Pacific as well as being a WPP board member. Both asked if I was available to assess the situation on the ground and give them my recommendations on the best course of action.

I headed straight for the agency's Bishop Street location in downtown Honolulu. What I found was complete chaos. Former employees were walking out of the building carrying client files and there was no one to stop them.

Looking around the lobby, I spotted the receptionist who had been with the agency when I was working there. I asked her what was going on. She said that the people taking the files said it was their client's property. I immediately locked the doors to the file area.

Then, I asked her if there was anyone else still on board. Her answer was straightforward. Besides herself, there were three bookkeepers, one copywriter, one art director, one broadcast producer and one junior account executive, who was on vacation.

Thinking on my Feet

While I was still trying to comprehend the magnitude of the situation, a well-dressed lady approached the receptionist. She said that she was the regional marketing director for our large containerized shipping client.

She had been notified that Ogilvy & Mather was closing the Hawaii office and she wanted to retrieve their advertising files and materials.

I hastily invited her to join me in the adjacent conference room where I explained there had been some miscommunication. At the time, I had no idea what inter-modal shipping meant. Nevertheless, I launched into my first client defense presentation and got her to agree to keep her business with us until things were sorted out.

> Without a larger, global anchor client, the future looked bleak.

I owed both Graham Phillips and Clif Kagawa my assessment. I told Mr. Phillips he should consider shutting the office down. It had initially been established to support the General Foods Asia/Pacific & World Trade Operations, which were headquartered in Honolulu. The acquisition of General Foods by Phillip Morris, and subsequent merger with Kraft Foods, had reduced the Hawaii operations to nothing more than a regional sales office.

Without a larger, global anchor client, the future looked bleak. The higher cost structure and business disciplines of a global advertising agency made it difficult to compete with smaller and nimbler local firms for locally-based business.

Closing Not an Option

Graham Phillips threw cold water on my recommendation. Only two years before, the Hawaii office had entered a long-term lease for a floor and half at their current location. Sir Martin Sorrell, the founder and CEO of WPP, wasn't keen on the idea of paying for unproductive real estate. My mission was to come up with another plan.

David Ogilvy had always said, "If you don't have an immediate idea or solution, open up a bottle of nice red wine and an idea will come!"

Being of Scottish descent, I had always subscribed to this common-sense approach. I observed the skyline of Waikiki was obscured by high rise hotels. At the time, the agency's client list included only two businesses in the tourism industry: the Polynesian Cultural Center, a visitor attraction on Oahu's north shore, and Hawaiian Airlines, who had filed for their second Chapter Eleven reorganization in a decade and owed the agency several million dollars.

A Travel Agenda

I reasoned if we refocused our efforts on the important Hawaii travel industry, we might be able to leverage Ogilvy & Mather's vast global network.

The good news was I had been exploring the idea of opening a boutique marketing advisory business in Honolulu with two of my former associates.

One of these former associates was Frank Haas, who had been my account management partner at Ogilvy & Mather. He was now running marketing for Jardine Matheson's far–flung Pizza Hut operations throughout the Pacific. Mr. Haas was hands–down, one of the best marketing minds in the Islands and had a real grasp of how the travel industry worked and what moved the sales needle. A product of Northwestern University, he had started his career with Leo Burnett in Chicago working on the Procter & Gamble account.

> ...if we refocused our efforts on the important Hawaii travel industry, we might be able to leverage Ogilvy & Mather's vast global network.

Phil Kinnicutt, who had received his MBA from the University of Hawaii, was formerly the vice president of communications for the largest energy company in the Islands, a former client, and a retail oriented marketer.

While our discussions hadn't progressed beyond the idea stage, this seemed like an ideal platform for the three of us to launch our idea. I ran the idea past Graham Phillips. *He liked it.*

About the same time, the advertising account of the prestigious Hawaii Visitors and Convention Bureau came up for review.

The Hawaiian Don Quixote

I proposed the agency marshal all of its resources and pursue the account. This Don Quixote–like idea met with a great deal of skepticism since we were in the middle of defending the remaining businesses we still had on the books.

Frank Haas and I jumped on a plane and flew to Los Angeles for a hastily called meeting with Jerry McGee, head of the Ogilvy & Mather Los Angeles office, and his creative and media teams.

Following the meeting, Graham Phillips went out on a limb to support our efforts by committing the agency's financial resources to underwrite major, proprietary research in California, Hawaii's largest source market, and warm weather destinations throughout Mexico, where travelers had chosen those beaches over Hawaii's.

He also funded an extensive travel agenda where we met with key travel distribution partners, including airlines, rental car companies, retail travel agencies, travel wholesalers, and Ogilvy & Mather clients such as American Express and Shell Oil.

A New Kind of Travel Agency

The result? Just prior to the Agency's Annual Christmas Party, we received the news we had been selected as the

Agency of Record for Hawaii Visitors and Convention Bureau. A few short months prior to this win, the office had been near closing.

During the following twelve months, the office had an unprecedented string of business wins. Those included winning agency reviews for the Polynesian Cultural Center and Oahu Visitors Bureau, seeing Hawaiian Airlines through its reorganization and retaining the business, and earning the Pizza Hut Asia/Pacific business. With a simple course correction, the struggling office in Hawaii had become the largest advertising office in the region and a respected, global travel practice.

This impressive turnaround was major news in the Islands and the advertising industry. The topic made the cover of the *Hawaii Business Magazine*.

> With a simple course correction, the struggling office in Hawaii had become the largest advertising office in the region…

Setting Course Corrections

If I had learned this rule earlier, perhaps my retail venture would have succeeded. A similar concept that started after Kula Bay did just that. Rather than incur the high costs associated with building brick–and–mortar retail locations, Tommy Bahama built a lower cost, wholesale business first. Then, using those proceeds, they anchored their concept with strategic retail locations.

The solution was clear. For three years, Kula Bay shirts had been the featured Father's Day item for Nordstrom in major warm weather markets.

This targeted wholesale business was profitable, but it didn't fit with my initial concept.

Since experiencing this business setback, I had counseled my account teams and marketing departments to realize any smart, business school graduate can author a good, creative business plan.

But, it is the nimble executive who can recognize a potential problem once you go to market with a plan and then have the courage to chart a profitable course correction, who will be rewarded.

Why this Applies Today

This advice is particularly applicable in today's, ever-evolving technology world. Some companies cling to legacy businesses, while their competitors recognize an emerging trend and reinvent the space.

After years of continuing to rely on an internet-based declining revenue model, Yahoo was forced to auction off this once-lucrative enterprise to Verizon. Twitter has brought back a founder as CEO to make its initial concept more user-friendly and relevant as a real-time news source and reignite user growth.

Meanwhile, the legacy-based business model at Microsoft is being reinvented as an enterprise model based in the cloud. Most recently, Microsoft moved to further redefine this global enterprise positioning by acquiring LinkedIn and their growing corporate recruitment services capabilities. Apple is invading the software based business within the automotive industry. Winners aren't afraid to make a course correction.

Kula Bay came to life getting cover stories and winning industry awards, but was ill–fated as the first Gulf War and California's economic slump caused a meltdown in travel. Knowing what I do now, a course correction would be my prescription.

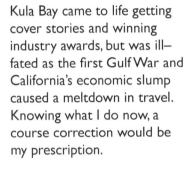

Left: Graham Phillips, former CEO of Ogilvy & Mather Worldwide

Right: Jerry McGee, Head of Ogilvy & Mather Los Angeles

Left: Phil Kinnicutt

Right: Frank Haas

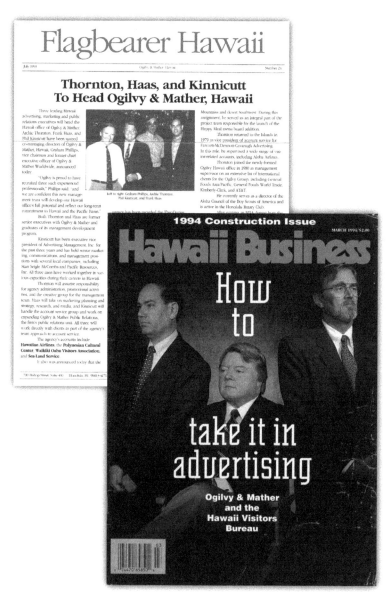

Top: Newsletter announcing O & M new management team

Bottom: The news is out: The impressive turnaround of
Ogilvy & Mather's Hawaii office made the cover of
Hawaii Business magazine.

Pictured left to right: Frank Haas, Archie Thornton, Phil Kinnicutt

Chapter Twelve

Don't Get Stuck in Silos

"In order for collaboration to take place, managers must give up their silos and their perceptions of power."

—Jane Ripley
Collaboration Begins with You: Be a Silo Buster

After helping right the ship in Hawaii, I was tapped to run the new travel division group of accounts operating out of Ogilvy's Los Angeles office. Many people don't realize that travel and tourism is the largest industry in the world, and a great source of outside income for many cities, resort destinations, and smaller developing countries. But the source markets for most of these destinations are spread out over wide number of geographic areas. This single factor makes it difficult for most resorts and destinations to reach their potential visitor with any consistent, concentrated advertising message or promotional offer.

Card Spending Secret

Over lunch with a regional manager of our American Express Travel Related Service client, I learned they had recently conducted a card member spending analysis.

The results revealed most card members used their American Express card like a cash management tool. With the two exceptions of Christmas and Valentine's Day, if a card member spent $1000 or $3000 a month on personal expenses such as gasoline, groceries, apparel, etc., then that amount was what the card member spent every month, give or take a few dollars.

> ...most card members used their American Express card like a cash management tool. The revealed spending patterns ... represented a very big opportunity.

This use of American Express's card member spending data is an early analog example of how important information gathering was then; and how increasingly important it will become in the evolving digital world. This will be addressed in more detail in Chapter Fourteen.

The only way to get a card member to significantly increase their spending pattern was to get them to travel, whether on business or leisure. The rationale was rather simple. When traveling, most people tend to suspend reality and indulge themselves with more expensive dinners, entertainment events, or purchases of apparel, jewelry, and gifts.

The spending patterns revealed in the study made common sense, and also represented a very big opportunity. Maybe we could find a way to use American Express support to increase the impact of the advertising and promotional efforts for some of our travel destination clients.

How to Make It a Win-Win

Naturally, the biggest beneficiary of any increase in card member spending would be the green, gold or platinum card groups. But, most of their budgets were allocated to card acquisition programs. They did have a smaller, strategic fund for targeted opportunistic programs. Unfortunately, if we spread this budget across different destination campaigns, the resulting impact would be minimal.

> The only way to get a card member to significantly increase their spending pattern was to get them to travel, whether on business or leisure.

There were other operating units that would benefit from any travel spending by card members. The most obvious was the American Express Travel offices and their preferred wholesalers, the travel industry distribution partners that packaged airline travel, hotel stays, and rental car use into a single price, leisure travel offering. But, their marketing efforts were retail-oriented and supported almost exclusively through local newspaper advertising in the Sunday Travel Sections.

Managing from Silos

Like in so many large corporations, the executives and managers of these distinct and separate silos were rewarded solely on the performance of their individual operations and not for their ability to work with the other groups to jointly promote their products.

It was our challenge to try and overcome this major hurdle and see if we could use the combined strength of these operating divisions to help drive card travel spending. But, I needed some compelling reason or glue to pull them all together.

> …we would identify strategic destinations that tended to attract more high–impact travelers—those that stayed longer and spent more money…

Partnering with our Partners

The solution was right under our nose. It was with our merchant services partners. Airlines, hotels, regional and national restaurant chains, rental cars, and major retailers all earned co-op dollars that they could spend to jointly promote their products or services when they accepted the American Express Card. We could now bring some real dollars to the table.

In conjunction with the card management, we would identify strategic destinations that tended to attract more high–impact travelers—those that stayed longer and spent more money on attractions, dining out, resort wear or gifts, and sightseeing tours. This combination would generate more card fees from the destination and encourage more merchants to accept and promote the use of the card.

Agency Boots-on-the-Ground

The sell–in was more like launching a military campaign than developing a cooperative promotion. A team comprised of American Express regional managers and my travel group team would approach the targeted Visitors and Convention

Bureau with a very compelling offer. If the destination would underwrite and support a destination-wide, cooperative promotional program with a commitment of, for example, $500,000, American Express would commit $300,000 in strategic funding to develop an integrated, travel promotion worth between three and five million dollars.

> A team comprised of American Express regional managers and my travel group team would approach the targeted Visitors and Convention Bureau with a very compelling offer.

High-impact Inserts

The typical program targeted the top four to eight major source markets for the destination. The destination promotional message was delivered in multiple-page inserts in regional editions of magazines covering those major source markets. The structure for the magazine inserts never varied.

Insert Timing

These promotions tended to be timed to drive travel to the destinations during their traditionally weaker shoulder periods while still supporting awareness and promoting advance bookings for the key travel seasons.

Blue Box Strategy Success

The strategy became generally recognized as the *Blue Box Strategy for Travel*. Since most destinations are partially or wholly supported by government funding, accountability was always an overriding concern. Accordingly, we designed this program to have a built in call–to–action so monitoring the results of the promotion and its return on investment was simple and credible.

Strategic Partnerships for Success

In today's world, many marketers view their distribution or retail partners for their products or services strictly as customers. And if they do, this type of relationship can deteriorate into an almost adversarial situation where each party perceives that the other is only concerned with their company's own self–interest and bottom line results.

When this type of environment exists, the distributors or retailer can appear to only be interested in negotiating the lowest price for those goods or services, securing the on time delivery of those goods or services, accessing the highest quality of customer support, and benefiting from their advertising and marketing support.

> In the digital world, technological success is built on a foundation of partnerships and strategic relationships.

Meanwhile, the manufacturer or service company people can start to feel like they are doing all the work—from product development and innovation, to paying for shelving allowances, and providing the promotional support to drive sales. In their minds, the major portion of the benefits is reaped by the distributer or retailer as a result of their effort.

This arm's length association, or "silo mentality," is not healthy for either party's ongoing success. In the digital world, technological success is built on a foundation of partnerships and strategic relationships. The successful technology innovators have come to the realization that renaissance men are in short supply today and no specific technology can solve every problem. So, instead of embracing the costly and time consuming approach trying to reinvent the wheel, successful technology companies have learned the quickest path to a satisfactory solution usually involves identifying the right partner(s) to help provide those tools and means for the goal.

> …recognize that your best promotional partners are most often your existing customers.

When I see a company pursuing high–cost, marketing initiatives, such as movie tie–in promotions and product placement costs, football halftime events and concert tours, or high–priced celebrity spokespersons without integrating a retail or channel marketing component to leverage that investment, I can only assume their goal is not to invest in building their brand(s) or generating returns for their shareholders but, rather for the self–aggrandizement of the marketing department.

Over the years, I have learned that the best way to support your brand and move the sales needle is to recognize that your best promotional partners are most often your existing customers. Not only will their integration strengthen the results of your investment efforts, it will build a better relationship that will benefit you and your distribution and retail partners, as well as your ultimate customer.

The insert cover delivered a positioning message consistent with the destination's brand image, and American Express logo.

The insert back cover promoted travel package offers at the featured accommodations. The call–to–action was a 1–800 number to an informed call desk with American Express or a preferred wholesaler.

The interior content promoted:

- The sponsoring airline's convenient connections
- The easy ways to explore the destination using the rental car promotional partner
- And the many ways to see and use the destination by calling out attractions on a map or listing participating restaurants, retailers, or sightseeing—all using co–op earned funds.

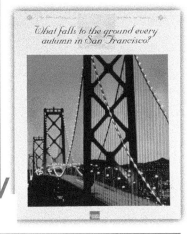

The structure for the magazine inserts never varied. Opposite is an example of an early insert for Maui; above is a later insert promoting San Francisco.

Ogilvy & Mather

MEMO

Date: June 3, 1996

To: O&M Hawaii Partners

Official Announcement

What we have expected for sometime has finally been confirmed by the leading advertising industry publication, *Advertising Age*, in their June 3rd edition.

From this day forward, Archie Thornton is THE Ogilvy & Mather Tourism Ad Expert. So it is written!

Funding crunch revamping travel ads

As gov't dollars dry up, integrated programs arise

By Alice Z. Cuneo

[SAN FRANCISCO] Reductions in state and federal funds are putting pressure on ad agencies to construct integrated travel and tourism programs, Ogilvy & Mather tourism ad expert Archie Thornton told a group of California marketers recently.

"Travel programs, not just ads—that's what the industry is buying today," said Mr. Thornton, who as international management director-travel group heads the Hawaii Visitors Bureau account at Ogilvy & Mather, Honolulu. Mr. Thornton spoke here at the northern California chapter of the Travel & Tourism Marketing Association.

As the federal government shifted responsibility for some entitlement and welfare programs to the states, states have become hard-pressed to maintain travel funding, Mr. Thornton said.

POLITICAL PRESSURES

"How can an assemblyman justify bankrolling the big hotel and airline industries when he is presiding over the rollback of social programs in his district?" Mr. Thornton asked.

As a result, states have cut their budgets for tourism ads. Hawaii's has been sliced 56.3% since 1991 to $3.5 million last year, and now requires that all public funds spent on marketing be matched by private industry.

The result, he said, is one 30-second TV spot for Hawaii, for example, that included two destinations, an airline, a retail price offer, a travel planner offer, a toll-free phone number and logos.

Other states, such as Florida and California, are moving in the same direction, Mr. Thornton said, while the federal government just eliminated the U.S. Travel & Tourism Administration.

Overall ad spending in the U.S. for travel, hotels and resorts rose 12% in 1994 to $2.3 billion, according to *Advertising Age's* "100 Leading National Advertisers" report. □

A division of The Ogilvy Group Inc., 11766 Wilshire Boulevard · 9th Floor · Los Angeles, CA 90025-6538 · Telephone 310-996-0400 · Fax 310-996-0698

This is a memo sent from the Los Angeles management to the Hawaii office after *Advertising Age* reported on one of my speeches at a Travel Industry event in San Francisco.

Chapter Thirteen

Digital Pitfalls and Road Bumps

"See into the future or become digital road kill!"

—Peter Jay Sorenson
CMC Owner, Strategic Organization Design

The Trip Down the Digital Highway

There is no express lane to success in the world of technology start–ups. How did I find the roadmap to success and avoid all those pitfalls? The truth is, I didn't.

In the Hawaii office, we had assembled a stellar creative team to support our burgeoning travel portfolio of clients. What I didn't realize was one of our young creative teams also shared a passion for software and its role in new, emerging technologies.

At the time, our Los Angeles office was the lead agency for Microsoft. Finding technology–oriented creative teams in these early days was a daunting task. When the special talents of our team emerged, we were inundated with project assignments from our much larger, West Coast sibling.

It was the late 1990s. The management baton for the Hawaii office was passed to my managing partner, Frank Haas, as I was relocating to the Los Angeles office to manage the newly formed travel group of clients.

Prior to the move, my wife Gail and I had planned a grand tour of Europe for our honeymoon. We received an invitation from David Ogilvy to visit him and his wife Herta at his chateau in Touffou. It was to be one of the highlights of our trip.

We planned to spend three days in Paris before driving down to Touffou. It was early in the morning on the second day, when I received a call from the managing director of the Paris office. He had been asked to give me a call to brief me before some pending news hit the business press.

His message was straightforward. "Archie, I wanted to alert you that today, Ogilvy will be announcing that we are resigning the AT&T, Compaq Computers, and Microsoft advertising accounts."

These were three, major blue–chip pieces of business. My first response was, "Do I still have a job?"

He was very reassuring. "Don't worry. At the same time, we will be named as the worldwide agency for IBM." The IBM account's annual billing was more than double that of the combined budgets of the other three accounts. We would be replacing more than forty individual agencies spread around the world.

Technology 101

After the relocation to Los Angeles, I found myself immersed in a frenzy of IBM activity. To replace the lost billing from the Microsoft account, the Los Angeles office had been assigned the software portion of the massive IBM business. I could witness, firsthand, the impact technology was going to have on my world.

A Leap into the Unknown

Technology and the internet were rapidly changing the world and I wanted to be part of the revolution. It was an entrepreneurial frontier. In 1997, I decided to retire from Ogilvy & Mather and set out on my own.

The Thornton Works Beginnings

I founded a new one man firm, The Thornton Works, Inc. to keep the lights on. I continued to provide some strategic consulting services for several blue–chip clients such as American Tool (makers of Vise–Grip), Convex Entertainment, Hawaiian Airlines, and TEAM Unlimited (parent company of the XTERRA Off–Road Triathlons and trail running series). But, the primary focus of my consulting firm was to try and get my arms around where technology was heading and how I could be a part of it.

I was not an engineer, so programming was not in the cards. What I could contribute was a lifetime of major advertising and marketing experience.

Travelago...a No–Go

My first major foray into the technology space was with a Kentucky based, start–up on the cutting edge of video streaming.

The company was Travelago Inc., a pioneer in providing streaming, travel planning content to online travel sites. The concept was simple and straightforward.

The Thornton Works played a leading role in securing early stage seed capital, managing subsequent rounds of financing, and launching a new video streaming service to the travel industry. I was named Chief Executive of this new company because of my experience in travel and tourism and my contacts within the industry. I led this new venture from 1999 until early 2001.

> ...we were a victim of being too early and became another road kill casualty littering the roadside of the technology highway.

Solution Outpaced Technology

At Travelago, I learned a very valuable lesson. Technology can get ahead of the marketplace. Our product, technology, and strategy were fine.

Unfortunately, we were years ahead of the infrastructure. Dial–up was still the dominant internet provider and the pipes for the limited DSL and cable services were just too restrictive to deliver our videos.

Marc Andreesen, the software pioneer, successful co-founder, and general partner of the Andreesen Horowitz Venture Capital Firm, has been an outspoken advocate of not being too early when it came to investing in potentially disruptive businesses. At Travelago, we were a victim of being too early and became another road kill casualty littering the roadside of the technology highway.

SmartDisc...Not the Smartest Timing

My next venture was in the anti–piracy for movies. During my stint managing the travel group of clients out of the Los

Angeles office, I had done some promotional project work with the account team for Paramount Studios. The Academy Award–winning film *Titanic* was among the number of films we helped launch. During this period, I built relationships with major players within the movie industry. The law firm for The Thornton Works, Inc. was Manatt, Phelps & Phillips, who had a major entertainment practice.

A Canadian technology start–up approached me to help them introduce their new, anti–piracy technology to the movie industry and develop a go–to–market strategy. I assembled an experienced team of industry veterans.

We spent over two years working with major studios such as Warner Bros. and industry groups like the Motion Picture Association of America.

This breakthrough technology, which incorporated a flash chip embedded in a two–part, slip–disc DVD, proved to be a potentially potent anti–piracy tool. Unfortunately, production and implementation hurdles delayed introduction of the technology until the train had left the station.

Solution to a Non–Problem

In this instance, instead of being too early to the party, we were just too late to find a solution to a problem that was at the end of its technology product lifecycle. The DVD home video distribution model was migrating to the new video streaming capabilities.

> Technology is a living, breathing phenomenon designed to feed on itself with advances regularly leapfrogging the standards of the moment.

Hard Learned Technology Lessons

So, what's the purpose of pointing out these personal examples of digital roadkill?

These examples demonstrate how any hot technology craze of the moment may be nearing the end of its meaningful product life. Technology is a living, breathing phenomenon designed to feed on itself with advances regularly leapfrogging the standards of the moment.

> Today's marketers cannot become complacent with simply deploying a functioning website, delivering improved search engine optimization, and developing an extended network of online resellers.

Gordon E. Moore, the co–founder of Intel, predicted in a paper he published in 1965 that the number of transistors on an integrated circuit could, and would, double every couple of years—and at a reasonable cost. What he was describing here, in what was to become known as Moore's Law, was the ability and reality for rapid advancements in technology to provide the foundation and capabilities to fuel human advancements. Such a foundation will provide the capabilities to revolutionize human productivity, create genetically engineered cures for disease, and improve living conditions in the developing world.

On a much more focused scale, the same rapid evolution will shape the marketing tools of tomorrow. When I first entered the internet environment, the watchword for cutting-edge media centered around landing pages, banner ads with links, and rich media.

Over time, this has evolved into integrated social media strategies incorporating blog celebrities, YouTube producers, and narrowly focused news and lifestyle sites.

Today's marketers cannot become complacent with simply deploying a functioning website, delivering improved search engine optimization, and developing an extended network of online resellers. Marketing opportunities will continue to evolve, become more refined, and deliver more targeted results by employing data mined through advances in artificial intelligence capabilities.

> ...we must continuously explore, evaluate, and embrace new technological tools. You want to be one of the disrupters and not one of the disrupted.

I predict it may not be long before the reliable internet browser we have come to rely on is replaced by voice activated, in–home devices such as Amazon's Alexa, Echo, Google's Home, or similar entertainment based components that provide easily accessible data or management of the internet–of–things. This is just one of many new technology advancements that will reshape our world.

For our marketing efforts to remain relevant and productive, we must continuously explore, evaluate, and embrace new technological tools. You want to be one of the disrupters and not one of the disrupted.

After living through these promising, but disappointing experiences, *I took a step back and tried to rethink my strategy and approach.*

Course Correction

I decided that I would morph The Thornton Works into a boutique, venture capital company and advisory firm. Under this new business model, I would continue to focus my efforts on identifying disruptive technology opportunities. I could then leverage my industry experiences and contacts in the advertising, apparel, entertainment, and travel industries.

Instead of providing consulting or interim management services, I would focus my efforts on identifying and investing in new companies and technologies that I was confident would be successful.

The next chapter will look at how one start-up will transform everyday life and directly impact the world of media.

An eye–catching advertisement for the now defunct *Travelago*

```
                    F A X

TO: ARCHIE THORNTON        DATE:  26 APRIL, 1994

FM: DAVID OGILVY           PAGES:  ONE (This one)

- - - - - - - - - - - - - - - - - - - - - - - - - - - - - - -

We shall expect you two for lunch on May 27.  Hurrah!

Touffou is in Bonnes, about 20 kilometres south of
Chatellerault.



                    David
```

Mr. Ogilvy's invitation to visit his chateau in France

Chapter Fourteen

There's a Tsunami Coming

"Immersive Virtual Reality...is a Tsunami coming. It will be as transformative as the P.C., then the Internet, and then, mobile."

—Michael Yanover
Head of Business Development,
Creative Artists Agency

I believe we will witness advances in technology we couldn't have imagined when I first became involved in the industry.

At the core of this transformation are new, improved capabilities in collecting, aggregating, and analyzing vast quantities of big data, now generally referred to as *artificial intelligence.* Utilizing this new resource, marketers can more accurately predict human purchasing or behavioral traits. Marketers can then adapt their product or service offerings to address these trends and refine their messages and choice of media to reach this more targeted customer.

Earlier in the book, I showed how the valuable data revealed in the American Express card member study opened the door to major promotional opportunities. They were extending a valuable, and soon to be expected, critical component of what would become today's digital toolbox: Data collection and analysis. The ideas and marketing possibilities were limitless then with customer data like American Express was able to provide. The opportunities remain the same today, only getting access to the data has become much easier and faster.

Blockchain, the ledger–based technology platform, promises to speed and simplify most transactions, while introducing a new level of anti–hacking security. This is not possible with today's internet security, firewalls, or password protections. While the jury is still out on the potential success and acceptance of the cryptocurrencies that introduced this new system, its underlying technology promises to make the internet as we know it obsolete.

Other major advancement will come in chip design. I believe the next generation of chips, which will employ molecular circuitry, will have the capability to mimic the human brain and fuel rapid advancement in autonomous vehicles, medical discoveries, and the promised integration of the internet–of–things.

> …the real potential for life altering advances will be led by the early adapters within the industrial and medical fields.

As stated previously, virtual reality technology has the potential to usher in the Fourth Industrial Revolution. While the media has highlighted the potential in sexier aspects of the technology, evident and imbedded in electronic gaming or entertainment products, the real potential for life–altering advances will be led by the early adapters within the industrial and medical fields.

This exciting virtual world will depend, to a certain degree, on the practical advancements in evolving hardware. Products such as headsets that are lighter and hardened for industrial uses will have the power and battery life to deliver immersive solutions for business. These advances will be accelerated by 5G networks and the capacity, performance, and increasing longevity of the future generations of batteries.

In the future, companies will need to develop a complete library of *digital twins* of their existing products and components to access and redeploy research, product development, training, marketing, maintenance, and repair. Initially, the production of these digital twins will be outsourced to augmented and virtual reality studios with the expertise and production capabilities to produce images that meet or exceed the required tolerances and needs of that industry.

This new set of tools will require a completely new software platform, like that being deployed by Tsunami XR. Along with a proprietary content management system (or Enterprise Immersive Management) that can allow for secure storage, easy access, and real-time use and collaboration by engineers and marketers on a global basis.

> But, augmented and virtual reality, when coupled with predictive analytics, will change everything we do.

This evolution will transform our existing systems of research, development, training, maintenance and repair. These transformations will be accelerated and magnified by accompanying advances in artificial intelligence, robotics, biotechnology, and quantum computing.

In a base case scenario, Goldman Sachs estimates the software segment for augmented and virtual reality alone could reach $85 billion in revenue by 2025, and as much as $150 billion in a best–case scenario, if the technology advances as predicted.

Whether you are using these new tools to troubleshoot maintenance problems on a jet engine in a remote location, close a highly complicated sales process, or train a new service technician for a major utility company, these virtual or augmented reality capabilities will provide valuable business solutions that will speed product manufacture, improve quality control, minimize downtime, and strengthen customer relationships.

Revolutionizing All We Do

This disruptive technology will change the way we do things. The proliferation of online travel agencies have changed the way we plan and book travel arrangements. Uber and Lyft have democratized the taxi and ride sharing industry. Amazon and Alibaba have changed our modern day shopping habits. Search engines like Google streamlined our ability to find results.

These incredible advances in technology have addressed changing the way we live our lives. But when coupled with predictive analytics, augmented and virtual reality will change everything we do.

...early adopters will find new immersive tools that provide valuable solutions and can dramatically improve advertising effectiveness and drive sales results.

From birth, we learn from our surroundings and environment. It is a 360–degree world of information and experiences that provide our foundation for learning. It seems natural that we would achieve more and perform better in a learning and working environment that utilizes the tools that simulate this realistic setting.

How to Compete and Win in the Immersive World

Some people in the business world view augmented and virtual reality as toys for the entertainment and gaming world, or a distraction for business applications and solutions. These naysayers will find themselves playing catch up in the decade to come.

Marketers who become early adopters will find new immersive tools that provide valuable solutions and can dramatically improve advertising effectiveness and drive sales results.

Harness Big Data

Gone are the days of advertisers relying on the time consuming snapshots provided by exhaustive quantitative studies, or the more subjective, often misleading, results of qualitative methods such as focus groups. Finally, artificial intelligence is putting actionable data in the hands of marketers in real time.

> It is important businesses don't allow new data to become overwhelming.

Over the last two decades, the internet, along with computer-aided record keeping, has provided every level of business with the tools to generate complex customer data bases, purchasing histories, and product or services preferences.

Today, with the emergence of sensors embedded in the expanding internet-of-things world, GPS tracking capabilities, and supercomputer processing, artificial intelligence (big data) can provide a previously untapped wealth of knowledge for businesses. But, big data for data's sake can paralyze decision-making for businesses.

It is important businesses don't allow new data to become overwhelming. The best way to resolve this dilemma is by seeking out software tools that are available from many artificial intelligence providers and allow decision makers to visualize data in a real-time, dashboard environment and then turn that data into actionable information.

Visualization of real-time data will enable marketers to nimbly adapt their marketing message or delivery media to changing market conditions, weather patterns, pricing pressures, or competitive initiatives.

With this newfound ability, marketers will have a rapid, real-time reaction tool that translates into sales success.

Marketing Activation

During my career in advertising, I have seen many masterful, creative campaigns fail, or fall short of reaching their potential, because the marketing team failed to activate the positioning and message at the critical point-of-sale.

> Visualization of real–time data will enable marketers to nimbly adapt their marketing message or delivery media to changing market conditions…

Most marketing campaigns have traditionally been delivered to the field as a *fait accompli* without adequate interaction or meaningful dialogue with the sales team, distribution partners, suppliers, or customers. Part of the problem stems from the current legacy methods of enterprise communication or collaboration available.

In today's fast–paced business environment, the winners are businesses fast to market with a new product innovation or rapid response to changing consumer trends and market conditions.

Current legacy meeting tools such as email blasts, GoToMeeting, Skype, or WebEx sessions are not really designed for effective collaboration. Rather, they have been developed to allow a session leader to visually deliver a prepared presentation that may, or may not, be followed by a conference call discussion. I would recommend ditching these outdated methods for the new immersive collaboration tools that are rapidly becoming available.

New collaboration platforms, such as Tsunami XR's Workspaces, and meet.com embrace all forms of immersive technology, 3–D internet, and functionally interactive 2–D images. With these new platforms, meeting participants can converge in a custom created environment specially designed to enhance the team collaboration. For example, a fast food restaurant chain might find that the meeting to discuss potential store redesigns is more productive if the collaboration takes place in a simulated restaurant. Or, for a sports equipment manufacturer, the environment might want to simulate a sports field. The options are unlimited.

New collaboration platforms… …embrace all forms of immersive technology, 3–D internet, and functionally interactive 2–D images.

In these unique meeting environments, participants can engage with meeting tools they are familiar with, including JPEGs, white boards, and PowerPoint capabilities. But, in these new immersive environments, participants can now annotate, edit, and comment on content verbally with voice–to–text, or stylus tools. In addition, these new collaboration platforms will have the capability to ingest any meaningful CAD files, upload MPEGs, or access any web-based content.

With these platforms you can enjoy broader participation, produce faster decision–making, and reduce unneeded travel costs. The platform will be accessible by any device, including; virtual reality headsets, desktops, tablets, and IOS or Android mobile devices. For example, a financial manager having coffee in a Starbucks in Hong Kong would be able to participate in an automotive engineering meeting in Detroit via his iPhone.

In actual practice, many mid–sized and large companies suffer from what is often referred to as meeting redundancy. Simple decisions are often rehashed throughout regional offices, departmental silos, and supplier discussions or requests due to poor communication. These new platforms will provide a persistent or perpetual capability that captures and memorializes all comments, revisions, and decisions. Team members anywhere in the organization can follow the decision–making process and be in a position to act on those conclusions.

Virtual Training for Real Results

Sometimes, someone would misinterpret the meaning of our marketing message or campaign. I assumed the misinterpretation a failure on my part to adequately articulate the purpose or meaning of the messaging.

Lately, I have come to realize the problem was not with the message, but rather, the method. By employing a 360-degree virtual training environment, an employee learns faster and retains more than in a traditional classroom setting or communicated in a computer presentation.

To the non-marketing executives or small business owner who might see themselves as being technically challenged, the prospect of producing virtual reality training videos may seem like an impossible task.

Today's 360-degree cameras are affordable and advanced. The training video task is surprisingly simple. Engage one of your most capable and talented employees to demonstrate and film the correct way to complete a task, whether assembling a product, providing a service, or simply selling your product or service. The results will be stunning and the benefits long-lasting.

Putting Lessons to Work

As another way to ensure lessons see their way to the shop floor, many employers are reinforcing the lessons learned in the virtual reality environment. These are available and reproduced in an augmented reality form (by superimposing the step-by-step job instructions) available to employees on the lens of industrialized glasses or goggles. This simple approach improves quality control, increases employee productivity, maintains quality standards, and lowers overall costs.

Introduce Digital Twins to the Family

To many small businesses, the concept of creating digital twins of their products or retail spaces will seem expensive or unnecessary, without any meaningful benefit.

> Digital twins will become the foundation for creating responsive digital showrooms.

Today, Amazon is encouraging its retail partners to provide them with digital 3–D imagery for use on their site. Soon, it will be a requirement.

But, if you are not using Amazon as a sales or distribution partner, what is the benefit? These digital twins will become a key component in driving sales, building customer loyalty, enhancing customer support, and improving internal company collaboration.

Digital twins will become the foundation for creating responsive digital showrooms. These powerful new showrooms will enable companies to quickly update product offerings, modify the image of existing products, and adapt the showroom environment to reflect seasonal themes.

> It has been my experience that if you can create a PowerPoint presentation for your business, you will be able to build your digital twin library.

Separately, digital twins will help companies create tailor–made environments to reach loyal customers and strengthen the brand relationship.

Digital twins will also become an increasingly important component for a company's customer support operations when helping a customer work through an installation problem, solve a product assembly issue, or explain a technical use procedure. Internally, digital twins will be a valuable aid within new immersive collaboration capability.

So, how does a non–tech manager or small business owner go about creating this new family of digital twins? It has been my experience that if you can create a PowerPoint presentation for your business, you will be able to build your digital twin library.

Faro and Matterport are just two of the affordable and user friendly scanning devices that allow you to scan existing products. Then, using their recommended software, convert those scans into quality 3–D imagery. Other software options include Polyworks by 3–D Infotech or Recap by Autodesk.

Whether your company manufactures widgets or wallpaper, distributes tools or toiletries, or provides transportation services, it will be increasingly important for you to have a digital record or twin of each product you make, your retail space, or shipping container capacities.

> It is our responsibility to envision and embrace the possibilities that comes with each of these new digital innovations…

In summary, use of these digital twins will help drive sales, strengthen customer relationship, and improve customer support services. They will also facilitate improved training, collaboration, and decision–making with consultants, suppliers, and department heads by enabling everyone to accurately visualize specific manufacturing problems, assess changes in sales floor layouts, and review a new product design alternative.

It is our responsibility to envision and embrace the possibilities that come with each of these new digital innovations and demonstrate a willingness to adopt tools to create better and impactful marketing programs.

The More Things Change...

The essential advertising lessons that I have learned focus on:

- The quality of our storytelling, or the way we structure content remains even more important on the expanded media canvas

- The need to refine and perfect our sales abilities

- The way we select media most appropriate to deliver our messages within this expanded, immersive environment

- The need to fully understand the distribution channels for our products or services

- The ability to learn from our successes, failures, and the courage to change course based on what we learn

The secrets introduced in this book will continue to serve as a solid foundation for advertising success in the evolving and immersive world of media.

Chapter Fifteen

Choose Your Mentors Well

"If the future strength of Ogilvy & Mather is to build on greater knowledge of advertising, then our knowledge must be systematically disseminated and taught."

—Bill Phillips
Chairman, Ogilvy & Mather

Next to my father, there were three men who had the most influence on my life and career. These three men were all members of our greatest generation, those who served their countries during World War II and helped win the war over tyranny.

John McDermott

My first mentor was also my first employer in advertising. His name was John McDermott. McDee, as I liked to call him, was a born leader of men.

During the invasion of Europe, his leadership role was recognized with a battlefield commission as major in the army. A true renaissance man, he remained in Paris after the war to work as a reporter and correspondent for the *International Herald Tribune.*

After career stops in New York and San Francisco, he worked his way to Hawaii where he partnered with Vance Fawcett's new advertising agency to form Fawcett McDermott Advertising. Initially located in the iconic Aloha Tower on Honolulu's harbor waterfront, this agency grew into one of the dominant firms in the Islands representing major airlines, banks and finance companies, public utilities, travel, and tourism accounts.

Mr. McDermott was also a believer in the promise of the younger generation. At one point, one–third of the agency was under the age of thirty. And, while he recognized the potential talent of the younger employees, he didn't leave developing this talent to chance.

Twice a month, Mr. McDermott would invite the younger members in one of the departments of the agency to a lunch meeting in his residence in the Hilton Lagoon Apartments overlooking Waikiki Beach. There, sitting on his floor dining on hot dogs and San Miguel beer, he would conduct informal training sessions where he posed marketing problems, shared advertising successes or failures, and helped provide advice and direction.

The year I decided to leave the agency and try my luck on the mainland stage, Mr. McDermott was named Ad Man of the Year in Hawaii. To commemorate the occasion, I had a street artist airbrush an "Ad Man of the Year" shirt with a caricature of him sipping a martini while sitting on the hood of a Rolls-Royce. Rather than ignore this youthful recognition, he had the shirt framed and displayed in his office. We remained close friends until his death in 2010.

John McDermott

Man of many facets, John McDermott also authored the book, *How to Get Lost and Found in New Zealand*

Chapter Fifteen: Choose Your Mentors Well

Richard Parker

I first met Richard (Dick) Parker a month after being hired by the H.D. Lee Company, the makers of Lee Rider jeans.

He had joined the New York office of Bozell & Jacobs to manage their newly acquired Lee fashion division account.

Mr. Parker was about twenty–five years my senior and had enjoyed a long and successful advertising career within the textile and apparel industries, most notably as head of corporate communications for industry giant, the J.P. Stevens Company. Among his many achievements was pioneering the promotional use of movie tie–ins.

Mr. Parker had been hired by the agency before my predecessor had announced his retirement.

Chuck Peebler, the agency president, was concerned our age gap would become an issue. He flew to Kansas City to volunteer to find a younger replacement. I put an immediate stop to the replacement option.

After only a few weeks on the job, I recognized I would need wise counsel and advice if I hoped to navigate the corporate world. Mr. Parker proved to be exactly what I needed. Over one of our early business lunches, he asked about my initial title as advertising manager. He suggested it sounded old–fashioned and not worthy of my responsibilities. He recommended I consider changing my title to advertising director. I asked, "How can I go about doing that?" He said simply, "You print the business cards, don't you?"

After that, we would talk by phone daily. I could confidentially share my problems and concerns, float ideas, and get suggestions on how to survive company politics.

In New York, we would spend hours visiting major retail stores where he would point out marketing successes and failures in garment labeling, store displays, and promotions.

He introduced me to major players in both the textile and fiber industries and explained how we could leverage those relationships to support our efforts.

But most importantly, he became a lifelong friend. I even named my youngest son after him. A graduate of the Rhode Island School of Design, Richard Parker is still active as both a watercolor artist and writer. In addition to his many published articles, he recently authored the book, *The Improbable Return of Coco Chanel*, where he chronicled his days as her assistant during the opening of her flagship fragrance showroom in New York after the war.

Mr. Parker had served in the Pacific theatre during World War II and was part of the occupying forces in Japan. While stationed on the Island of Kauai, he secured some Japanese pen and ink supplies from a local general store and on some plain brown wrapping paper he found, captured the magic and mystery of the Island's Na Pali cliffs. His pen and ink artwork is one of my most treasured possessions.

The Improbable Return of Coco Chanel by Richard Parker

Pen and ink by Richard Parker

Richard Parker

David Ogilvy

During World War II, David Ogilvy worked under Bill Stephenson on Project Ultra, the Allies' undertaking to break the German Enigma Code. The painstaking attention to detail and teamwork required in this effort carried over to the corporate culture at Ogilvy & Mather.

D.O., as he would come to be known within the agency, firmly believed:

> "Training should not be confined to trainees. It should be a continuous process and should include the entire professional staff of the agency. The more people learn, the more useful they can be to our clients." From the agency publication, "Principles of Management."

It didn't matter which office I was working in. Every couple of months, a video arrived that was considered mandatory viewing for the staff. In these video tapes or "Magic Lanterns" training aids, David Ogilvy would present his views on the state of advertising, management principles, recruiting and hiring practices, the need for research, his disdain for company politics, and training.

In one presentation, Ogilvy said, "A company that is doubtful about its future doesn't bother to train. A company that has no unique point of view also finds training a waste of time." Even in semi–retirement, he never missed an opportunity to share his experiences and lessons learned. During our honeymoon visit with Mr. Ogilvy and Herta at his chateau in Touffou, he asked about the creative direction we were recommending for our newly acquired Hawaii Visitors and Convention Bureau account.

During our discussion, he excused himself to retrieve

some samples of early work he had done for both Britain and Puerto Rico. His eyes lit up with excitement as he recalled the success of both campaigns. It turned out the lower dungeon of the chateau was a treasure chest of samples of the agency's creative work over the years.

When we finished our discussions regarding destination advertising, he asked what the rest of our travel plans entailed. I told him the next major stop on our honeymoon was the Hotel Cipriani in Venice, but we weren't scheduled to check in there for three more days. Our plan was to take the back roads there and explore some of the small villages along the way.

He was aghast. He disappeared again, only to reappear with his arms full of Michelin Guides and rolled up maps. Dropping to his knees on the floor, he rolled out one of the maps and handed me a yellow notepad, said, "Take notes!"

He personally mapped out our travel itinerary for the next few days, including recommending several restaurants and chefs along the route. After walking us to our car, he tapped on the window. His parting comment was, "You owe me a commission on the hotel bookings."

He believed management had no monopoly on great ideas. Nor did creative people. Some of the best ideas can come from account executives, researchers, or media planners. And, he stressed it was important to encourage such involvement and innovation. Mr. Ogilvy said, "Change is our lifeblood, stagnation our death knell."

He stayed true to these ideals until his death in 1999.

Standing with David Ogilvy in
front of his Chateau de Touffou
in France

Postscript

My Personal Secrets to Success

- Never, ever Retire
- Listen to the Voices of Experience
- Surround Yourself with Smart, Young People
- Try to Learn Something New...Everyday
- Keep Trying to Change the World!

About the Author

Archie Thornton's successful marketing career has spanned more than four decades, including two stints with Ogilvy & Mather Worldwide, working with the legendary David Ogilvy.

While at Ogilvy, he served as Managing Director on the Asia/Pacific & World Trade Divisions of packaged goods giant, General Foods, and later managed the Global Travel Group, which included the American Express, Hawaiian Airlines, and Hawaii Visitors Bureau accounts.

Prior to joining Ogilvy & Mather, he served as the Worldwide Advertising Director for VF Corporation's Lee Riders apparel brand.

During an interlude from advertising, he founded and managed an upscale, men's tropical clothing chain with stores in California, Florida & Hawaii.

Today, he is a venture capitalist, a technology innovator and investor, and frequent speaker at technology events.

CPSIA information can be obtained
at www.ICGtesting.com
Printed in the USA
LVHW051436130819
627474LV00001B/1/P